The Lost Arts
of
Modern Civilization

The Lost Arts
of
Modern Civilization

Mitchell Kalpakgian

TAN Books
Charlotte, North Carolina

Published by TAN Books. This book was originally published in 2009 by The Neumann Press. Revised edition with color corrections, cover design copyright © 2014 TAN Books.

ISBN 978-1-61890-661-8

Printed and bound in the United States of America

TAN Books
Charlotte, North Carolina
www.TANBooks.com
2014

Dedication

TO THE beloved people in my life—Armenian immigrant family members and dear friends in the neighborhoods of Milford, Massachusetts, in the 1940s and 1950s—who exemplified these lost arts of living well, introduced me to their exquisite pleasures, and practiced them as a way of life that made them deliciously good and irresistible, especially the members of the Khatchig Kalpakgian, David Kalpakgian, and Hagop Balian families, and my own wife Joyce and five children.

To the great writers of Western civilization—especially Homer, Jane Austen, Dr. Johnson, Mark Twain, Cardinal Newman—whose work teaches the importance of these traditional arts for a human civilization in which the goodness of hearts, the gift of friendship, the mirth of hospitality, the liveliness of conversation, the pleasure of pleasing, and the beauty of love flourishes to give ordinary life its enchantment.

To the great teachers and special friends in my life in whose company I most savored the taste, sweetness, and goodness of these humane arts again and again over a lifetime: Professors Quinn and Nelick from Kansas University, Dr. Robert Carlson and Mr. Herbert Mosher of Wyoming Catholic College, and loyal friends from Iowa—the Colella, Gilbert, Kharouf, Kuhn, Selgrade, Stroh, and Vitale families.

Preface

SAMUEL Johnson, the eminent Dr. Johnson and eighteenth century man of letters, wrote that "The only end of writing is to enable the readers better to enjoy life, or better to endure it." The practice of these traditional arts, now rare in the technological universe of video culture, internet, e-mail, and electronic media, accomplish this very purpose of making daily life and ordinary routine more enjoyable or more endurable. These arts of living—the custom of hospitality, the habit of letter writing, the delight of conversation, the enjoyment of people, the desire of pleasing, and the practice of courtship— fill common life with an abundance of simple pleasures that adorn day to day existence.

They lift the spirit, rejoice the heart, whet the sense of mirth, and enliven the mind so that man's daily regimen of toil receives the food and medicine of laughter, lightheartedness, and pure fun to overcome the demons of melancholy, dullness, and world weariness that afflict the joyless who live only to work instead of working to live and living to enjoy life. Without the charitable way of life these traditional arts instill, persons lose the personal touch, the appreciation of the simple

pleasures, and the companionship of normal sociability, prefer-
ring instead interaction with technology rather than exchange
with a thinking, feeling, talking, loving, and laughing human
being full of life.

These traditional arts cultivate in persons a desire to give
and be generous, to appreciate and be grateful, to please and
to be thoughtful, to think of the happiness of others and of
ways to bring joy into their lives, and to cherish the gift of a
person as a blessing from God. Without the habitual practice
of these lost arts, life soon develops into an Orwellian universe
notorious for its flatness, deadness, and coldness. In the words
from Orwell's *1984*, "It struck him that the truly characteristic
thing about modern life was not its cruelty or insecurity, but
simply its bareness, dinginess, its listlessness."

In a modern world that has deconstructed the family with
its network of joy-filled relationships and in a society that
spends more time before flat screens and television monitors
than in human interaction, these lost arts offer the special
touch, voice, and affection that bring the sweet kindness and
goodness of the human heart into all people's lives so that they
may enjoy life more or endure life better.

Contents

Contents

Acknowledgments

VERSIONS of four of these essays were first published in *New Oxford Review* (1069 Kains Avenue, Berkeley, CA 94706) and are reprinted here with the permission of editor Pieter Vree: "The Lost Art of Hospitality" (February 2001); "The Lost Art of Letter-Writing" (September 2004); "The Lost Art of Conversation" (January 2008); and "The Lost Art of Enjoying People" (October 2007). "The Lost Art of Pleasing" appears in the January (2010) issue of *Homiletic and Pastoral Review* (70 Lake Street, P.O. Box 297, Ramsey NJ). It is reprinted here with the permission of editor Kenneth Baker, S.J. The final two essays, "The Lost Art of Courtship" and "The Lost Art of Tasteful Dressing or Proper Attire," have not appeared in any other publication.

CHAPTER ONE

The Lost Art of Hospitality

THROUGHOUT the Odyssey Homer distinguishes between the civilized and the barbarians—those who practice the art of "living well" (Aristotle's phrase) like the Phaeacians and those who merely live in the sense of survival like the Cyclops. The rituals of hospitality mark the culture of the civilized as they honor the traveler and respect the sacred law of the gods in their gracious welcome of the visitor. Homer describes a typical banquet scene that epitomizes old-world hospitality:

> A maid came with water in a beautiful golden ewer and poured it out over a silver basin so that he could wash his hands. Then she drew a wooden table to his side, and the staid housekeeper brought some bread and put it by him with a choice of dainties, helping him liberally to all she could offer.

These Homeric feasts cultivate many virtues associated with the refinements of civilization: a reverence for the divine, the appreciation of beauty, and the habit of liberality. First, the host pours libations to the gods as an expression of gratitude for the gifts of food and drink and for the abundance of nature's

1

harvest. Hospitable occasions honor the gods for their favors and awaken the mind to a contemplation of the divine. Second, the banquet serves the traveler in an atmosphere that evokes beauty—"the beautiful golden ewer" and "the silver basin" reflect choice dishware made with the best materials and skilled craftsmanship. As Pericles said about the Greeks in his famous funeral oration, "We are lovers of the beautiful. . . ." Third, the host abounds in generosity in preparing the best foods and offering the heartiest portions. When Telemachus is a guest in Menelaus's home, the host spares nothing in accommodating all the human needs of the traveler: "Meanwhile a carver dished up for them on platters slices of various meats he had selected from his board, and put gold cups beside them." In these scenes of hospitality from the *Odyssey*, the participants savor the fruits of civilization that dignify and elevate human life beyond the wearisome struggle for survival. The civilized refine and adorn life with manners, rituals, and arts that create the art of living well and an appreciation for all of life's exquisite pleasures.

Reverence for the gods, love of the beautiful, and the outpouring of liberality, however, define only part of the occasion. The great banquets in the *Odyssey* also provide occasions for conversation and storytelling, an opportunity for learning. As Odysseus sojourns in Phaeacia with King Alcinous, he recounts his adventures with the Cyclops, the Sirens, and the Scylla and the Charybdis to a rapt audience intent on increasing their knowledge. The feast, then, creates an atmosphere for learning, for broadening one's mind, for acquainting one's self with understanding of men and manners, and for hearing of the adventures of other travelers. Entertainment or games also accompany the rites of hospitality as the king summons the bard: "And let our glorious bard, Demodocus, be summoned. For no other singer has his heavenly gift of delighting our ears whatever theme he chooses for our song." Thus the enjoyment of the feast calls to mind an important philosophical truth known to the civilized: Men work in order to play, leisure is the basis of culture, and the love of beauty and truth are liberal pursuits inherently desirable for their own sake. As Pericles explains in his funeral oration, "And we have not forgotten to provide for our weary spirits many relaxations from toil; we have regular games and sacrifices throughout the year; our homes are beautiful and elegant; and the delight we daily feel in all these things helps to banish melancholy."

After partaking of their "fill of the good things we have shared, and of the banquet's boon companion, the harp," King Alcinous invites Odysseus to participate in the Phaeacian Games: "Let us go out of doors now and try our hand at various sports, so that when our guest has reached his home he can tell his friends that at boxing, wrestling, jumping, and running there is no one who could beat us." The athletic contests offer "the perennial delight" of sports and the mirth of robust competition. The final touch that concludes the custom of hospitality is the performance of the graceful dancers that "filled Odysseus with admiration as he watched"—a sense of wonder in contemplation of the miracle of the beauty of art. Hospitality, then, moves both hosts and guests to participate in life's highest pleasures and deepest joys so that man does not live to work but works in order to live well and participate in the perennial delights of human life.

Hospitality provides for the essential human needs of body,

soul, mind, and heart. The combination of delicious food and drink, convivial conversation and marvelous tales, beautiful music and dancing, gracious manners and bountiful generosity, and fun-filled games and contests cheers the heart, uplifts the soul, exhilarates the body, and elevates the mind. This participation in the revitalizing leisure of hospitality cultivates a sense of "the sweetness of life" in all its pure joyfulness. As Odysseus remarks,

> I myself feel there is nothing more delightful than when the festive
> mood reigns in a whole people's hearts and the banqueters listen
> to a minstrel from their seats in the hall, while the tables before
> them are laden with bread and meat, and a steward carries round
> the wine he has drawn from the bowl and fills their cups. This,
> to my way of thinking, is something like perfection.

In the Greek art of hospitality, the soul gives thanks to the gods, the body partakes of sumptuous food and drink, the five senses marvel at the miracle of beauty, the spirit rejoices in the company and conversation of friendship, and the heart falls in love with the goodness of life.

As the practice of old-world hospitality declines and fast-food restaurants and pre-packaged frozen dinners replace the arts of entertaining and pleasing guests, the virtues of guests and hosts disappear and the civilized custom of the feast fades as an educational, cultural influence. When homes fail to provide festive occasions where the art of graciousness flourishes, manners decline and sociability suffers. Occasions of hospitality cultivate certain virtues in the host: the art of cooking as an act of love; the art of pleasing guests; the art of creating an attractive, cheerful inviting atmosphere; and a spirit of generosity and the joy of giving. These festive banquets also develop particular virtues in the guest: the ability to be convivial, pleasant, and gregarious; the willingness to be at home in the company of all ages; the practice of self-forgetfulness in taking an interest in the lives and experiences of others; the skills of courtesy and civil conversation. When homes cease to be to centers of hospitality, they function only as utilitarian places where transients "grab a bite," "hit the sack," and "watch the game." The cultivation of leisure, friendship, good cooking, and delightful storytelling are never learned if everyone is too busy, too tired, or too lazy to be the generous host or the gracious guest. When television, video games, and the internet are substituted for human interaction, the personal, human touch is lost, and the world becomes a colder, more alien place. Happy faces, hearty laughs, and lively conversations all act as humanizing influences wherever hospitality abounds.

Amid the civilizing influence of hospitality, human beings recognize their sense of belonging and overcome their isolation. Oneness and solidarity follow when people enjoy a common meal, tell their life stories, and enjoy one another's company. Old and young relate to one another, and the transmission of wisdom, traditions, and customs continues from one generation to another. These occasions engender educational experiences, "old birds teaching young birds how to fly," to use C. S. Lewis's phrase. These festive times of sociability provide lessons on the primary purposes of life—the meaning of giving and receiving, loving and being loved, teaching and learning. Everyone who has been treated with the kindness of hospitality is obligated to extend this virtue of welcoming guests as if they were gods in disguise. As Menelaus explains to one of his lords guilty of a

breach in courtesy for failing to invite wanderers into his pal-
ace: "Think of all the hospitality that you and I enjoyed from
strangers before we reached our homes. . . . Unyoke their horses
at once, and bring our visitors into the house to join us at the
feast." Hospitality is a universal virtue that civilizes and humanizes all people and creates a unity in the family of mankind.

In Hawthorne's story about Baucis and Philemon in *A
Wonder Book*, an elderly couple who epitomize the ideal of
hospitality, two Greek gods appear in disguise as they travel
through a village dressed as beggars. Because of their shabby
appearance the townsfolk unleash their dogs to snarl at them,
and unruly boys hurl stones at the travelers. Finding welcome
only at the humble cottage of Baucis and Philemon, the gods
are warmly received into the home of the elderly couple:
" 'Friends,' said the old man, 'sit down and rest yourselves
here on this bench. My good wife Baucis has gone to see what
you can have for supper. We are poor folks; but you shall be
welcome to whatever we have in the cupboard.' " Apologizing
for the sparse fare of milk, bread, cheese, and honey she serves
her guests, Baucis pours the last drop of milk from the pitcher.
To her amazement the god Quicksilver (Mercury) pours more
milk from the empty pitcher, constantly filling and refilling
the glasses. For their kindness in welcoming strangers, Baucis
and Philemon receive the gift of the miraculous pitcher which
always replenishes itself after it is emptied, "an inexhaustible fount of nectar"—a token of the god's gratitude for the
boundless generosity of the old couple. The natural and the
human assume supernatural proportions, for, as one of the
gods remarks, "An honest, hearty welcome to a guest performs
miracles . . . and is capable of turning the coarsest food to

nectar and ambrosia." The graciousness of hospitality exalts daily life and reveals a glimpse of heaven on earth as humans and gods mingle in an atmosphere charged with the presence of the divine. The miracle of the pitcher which always fills after it is emptied corresponds to the mystery of the hospitable heart that is never depleted of the generosity of love.

In Kenneth Grahame's *The Wind in the Willows*, hospitality is a way of life that cultivates true, enduring friendships. After spending an enjoyable spring day rowing on the river with Water Rat, Mole savors the picnic lunch prepared by his host consisting of ham, beef, French rolls, and lemonade, exclaiming in the overflow of his happiness, " 'O stop, stop,' cried the Mole in ecstasies: 'This is too much!' " After delighting in the freshness of spring, exploring the beauty of the river, and relishing the outdoor picnic, Mole finds himself at night sitting in a comfortable armchair by a merry fire in Rat's home listening to river stories. At bedtime "a terribly sleepy Mole had to be escorted upstairs by his considerate host, to the best bedroom, where he soon laid his head on the pillow in great peace and contentment, knowing that this new-found friend the river was lapping the sill of his window." In this episode hospitality consists of sharing life's purest blessings and simplest pleasures with others. Water Rat proffers to Mole his love of the river, his knowledge of boating, his delicious fare, his comfortable lodging, and his favorite river stories. Rejuvenating the spirit, hospitality keeps one young at heart, playfully fun-loving, and in love with life's adventures. In the enjoyment of hospitality, the world becomes a personal place and a domestic kingdom. The warmth of affection and the sentiments of the heart enkindled by Water Rat's fire and friendship overcome the feeling of alienation that Mole encounters in the hostile world of the Wild Wood where no one cares, no one is friendly, and no one welcomes travelers into the home.

Like the bright fire provided in Rat's parlor, Badger's hearty welcome also warms the hearts of his visitors. The contrast between the "cold and trackless Wild Wood left outside" and "the embracing light and warmth" of Badger's cozy home illuminates the difference between feeling at home in a friendly world and being lost and terrified in a cold universe. As Rat and Mole find comfort in Badger's abode, they appreciate its quintessentially earthy qualities: This is the home of true hospitality, a place where home-cooked food is deliciously abundant and where friends enjoy and entertain one another. The homespun, down-to-earth, weathered characteristic of Badger's dwelling appears in the "well-worn red brick floor" and in "a long table of plain boards placed on trestles." The baskets of eggs, nets of onions, and bundles of herbs hanging from the rafters capture the rustic simplicity and spirited life of the home:

> It seemed a place where heroes could fitly feast after victory, where weary harvesters could line up in scores along the table and keep their Harvest Home with mirth and song, or where two or three friends of simple tastes could sit about as they pleased and eat and talk in comfort and contentment.

These occasions of hospitality forge the bonds of friendship. During these festive times relationships grow and develop into lifelong attachments. Just as experiences of hospitality cultivate warm, generous, and grateful hearts, they also foster deep loyalties. Such friendships not only create opportunities for mutual enjoyment but also inspire reasons for mutual helpfulness. Rat comes to the assistance of Mole when he loses himself in the Wild Wood and confronts danger; Badger welcomes Rat and Mole when they are cold and wet from the snow; and Rat, Badger, and Mole befriend Toad when his home is infested with the stouts and weasels. Without frequent hospitality these deep, enduring friendships of a lifetime do not develop, and life is devoid of this special pleasure of friendship called "the wine of life" by Dr. Johnson.

As modern homes become more utilitarian and function only as places to eat and sleep in a "workaholic" society, as two-income families drive women from the home and reduce the time and energy available for hosting, and as entertainment outside the home replaces hospitality within the home, all human relationships suffer. While people may have many acquaintances and colleagues, true friendships are often absent because hospitality has become a lost art. The enjoyment of people loses its appeal and delight when homes fail to provide sociable occasions that renew old friendships and cultivate new relationships. Scenes of hospitality create an atmosphere that simplifies the complexities of life to its quintessential joys—eating, drinking, playing, laughing, conversing—and weaves a lighthearted magical spell that dispels gravity, melancholy, and world weariness. These convivial occasions of mirth illustrate G. K. Chesterton's quip that "Angels can fly because they can take themselves lightly" and that "laughter is a leap"—the perfect antidote to the gravity of seriousness. Hospitality lifts the weight of the world and gives to the human spirit the levity of comedy.

A final scene of hospitality from *The Wind in the Willows*

depicts Rat visiting Mole's home. The guest is charmed by the
quaintness of the house, a simple abode that good taste has
transformed into a work of art. The Gothic lettering above
the front door, the baskets with ferns hanging from the walls,
a garden-seat near the door, and the plaster statuary all invite
and captivate the visitor. Excited, Rat exclaims, "So compact!
So well planned! Everything here and everything in its place.
We'll make a jolly night of it!" Before long every item in the
home becomes a conversation piece, and Mole narrates some
of his family history. The two friends deepen their relationship as Mole touches on the most personal aspects of his life:
"How this was planned, and how that was thought out, and
how this was got through a windfall from an aunt, and that
was a wonderful find and a bargain, and how this other thing
was bought out of laborious savings and a certain amount of
'going without'." Thus hospitality provides an invitation to
experience the depths and riches of another person, the chance
to enter into the drama, remarkable events, and surprising
changes in a person's life. As Rat enters Mole's home, he learns
of his friend's fondest memories, his dearest possessions, and
his greatest joys. Genuine hospitality takes the guest not only
into the inner sanctum of the home but also into the interior
chambers of the soul. The mystery of the person unfolds.

Without frequent occasions of hospitality, people remain
strangers and relate to one another only on the level of work
or business. They judge one another in terms of productiv-
ity, efficiency, and titles. They learn only superficially about
another person's background, family history, ethnic identity,
spouse and children—all natural topics of conversation in
a sociable, leisurely atmosphere. Only in the comfortable

surrounding of friends and in the relaxed setting of a festive occasion do people express what they truly think, feel, and believe instead of talking in clichés and slogans or repeating the syndicated opinions of the media. Culture depends on the custom of hospitality—people sharing their life stories and communicating in the most personal of ways, maintaining contact with the essential and the real. Hospitality is rooted in the down-to earth and the homespun, not in the artificial or the counterfeit. Hospitality keeps people in direct contact with "the permanent things," the universal experiences, and the true, the good, and the beautiful.

Without the real enjoyment afforded by hospitality, mindless entertainment fills the vacuum, substituting fantasy for reality. The sophisticated replaces the simple, and the exotic and the expensive become the desirable sources of pleasure. In the various scenes of hospitality in *The Wind in the Willows*, the characters taste the real thing and experience deep contentment and peace. It is this deep peace that Homer captures in his portraits of hospitality that he equates with "something like perfection." It is the foretaste of Heaven that Baucis and Philemon offer their guests, the nectar and ambrosia that the Greek gods cite as they bless the couple "for treating the humblest stranger as if he were a brother." In his famous book about fishing, *The Compleat Angler* (1653), Izaak Walton recognized the role of hospitality in civilization: "Good company and good discourse are the sinews of virtue." Like King Alcinous, Baucis and Philemon, and the friends in *The Wind in the Willows*, the hospitable fisherman grasps this important first principle: The experience of hospitality is for everyone "a rest to his mind, a cheerer of his spirits, a diverter of sadnesse, a calmer of unquiet thoughts, a moderator of passions, a procurer of contentednesse; and that it begat habits of peace and patience, in those that profess'd and practis'd it."

Where true old-world hospitality abounds, one does not need Hollywood, the internet, cable television, video games, overpriced entertainment, fashionable restaurants, and countless social organizations to provide diversion and pleasure. There is more to life than these pastimes that rarely go beyond the momentary and the superficial. In contrast, the regal banquets in the *Odyssey*, the bountiful hearts of Baucis and Philemon, and the cheerful welcome of the homes in *The Wind in the Willows* lead to the heart of reality, to the enduring sources of happiness and peace, and to the abiding joys of goodness, beauty, and friendship that create culture and form the basis of civilization.

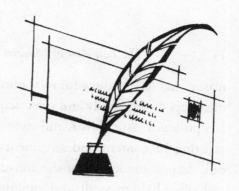

CHAPTER TWO

The Lost Art of Letter Writing

WHAT is one of the simplest, most inexpensive, and dearly cherished gifts a person can receive on nearly every given day of the year? It is of course not a special birthday present, a rare Christmas gift, or a unique collector's item. It is a personal letter. It is a simple gift because it does not require shopping or travel; it is inexpensive because it costs less than a dollar; and it is cherished because it possesses a permanent, enduring quality, something often carefully saved or preserved by its owner, As one collects his daily mail and recognizes the usual bills, the amount of junk mail, the credit card advertisements, special offers, and solicitations from various charitable organizations, a personal letter with distinctive handwriting and individual stationery sparkles as a prize or gem. As the world often becomes an inhospitable or dehumanizing place, a personal letter cheers and warms the heart and humanizes daily life. Life is not just business or work but play and delight, a friendly letter serving no utilitarian purpose but expressing an activity enjoyable for its own sake. As welcome as telephone calls are from family members and friends, nothing compares to a letter. Many favor letters to telephone calls for the simple reason that letters allow for re-reading and sharing with other members of the family and close acquaintances. Personal letters possess a taste, flavor, and style which lend themselves to savoring its content and sentiments. Somehow a telephone call, despite the length of the conversation, remains ephemeral, often hard to recall, and sometimes aimless or repetitious and never quite leaves as powerful an impression as a letter. While a telephone call reflects thoughtfulness and good will, it does not move or reach the heart with the same effect as the personal letter.

Why do letters always gladden the heart and lift the spirit so easily? Often they arrive as delightful surprises, some letters possibly beginning, "I bet that when you woke up this morning you never dreamt of receiving a letter from . . ." These surprising letters remind us that life is filled with unexpected gifts, strokes of good luck, and unforeseen occasions of hope. In receiving the gift of a letter, one is reminded that no one knows what will happen tomorrow. One recognizes that ordinary life transcends the prosaic and humdrum and that grace is present in daily experience. Father James Schall in *On the Unseriousness of Human Affairs* writes, "But the fact is that we seldom receive the letters we 'expect,' and often the ones we do not expect are the best ones we receive." In his essay "Letters and the Spiritual Life," he further explains: "The letter comes unexpectedly some morning or afternoon in the post. It bears that element of surprise, which is almost the deepest of our spiritual concepts." Thus personal letters reassure people that they are special, not social security numbers or anonymous creatures.

Someone found the time and took the interest and gave

priority to the importance of communicating to a friend, relative, or loved one; someone did not resort to the usual alibi of "I'm too busy" or "I don't have time"; someone realized the importance of the little things that beautify and civilize daily existence; someone still knows and practices the virtue of graciousness. A friendly letter testifies to the goodness of the human heart filled with kindness and affection.

The arrival of a letter, however, not only rejoices the spirit of the recipient but also expands the heart of the writer. The art of letter writing involves the practice of the presence of the other person. The writer must recall everything about the person being addressed—his character, temperament, sensibility, interests, and background—and imagine being in his company and holding a conversation with him. Letter writing cultivates in the correspondent the art of pleasing another person by engaging in common topics of interest, displaying a sense of humor, offering wise advice, acknowledging gratitude, or expressing love. Letter writing requires effort, concentration, and thought, even though it is often lighthearted, whimsical, and informal. One must find something to say that is substantive, engaging, or entertaining. In short, letter writing cultivates contemplation, an essential form of higher mental activity that transcends the mere exchange of information.

While greeting cards serve a purpose in celebrating all the special occasions of human life—birthdays, anniversaries, weddings, graduations, and funerals—they cannot replace the personal notes and deep emotions that a person's own words and sentiments communicate. For example, John Henry Newman's letter to Henry Manning just prior to the death of Manning's wife Caroline illustrates the comfort that a letter brings in a time of human tragedy when heart speaks to heart (*cor ad cor loquitur*):

> It often strikes me so when I am partaking of Holy Communion that I am but drinking in (perchance) temporal sorrow, according to His usual Providence. Hence St. Peter tells us not to think affliction a strange thing. Let us then, my dear Manning, be your comfort,—You are called to trouble as we all are, and the severer the more God loves you. . . . . He does not willingly afflict us, nor will put a single grain's weight more of suffering than it is meet and good for you to bear—and be sure too that with your suffering your support will grow, and that if in His great wisdom and love He take away the desire of your eyes, it will only be to bring her really nearer to you. For those we love are not nearest to us when in the flesh, but they come into our very hearts as being spiritual beings, when they are removed from us. Alas! It is hard to persuade oneself this, when we have the presence and are without the experience of the absence of those we love; yet the absence is often more than the presence, even were this all, that our treasure being removed hence, leads us to think more of Heaven and less of earth.

Because Newman writes to Manning as friend to friend speaking heart to heart, he does not offer false pity, pious clichés, or sentimental cant. The mystery of death and its inconsolable grief move Newman to speak from the depths of his soul and from the riches of his mind as he offers Manning all his human wisdom and spiritual consolation. The beloved is not eternally absent but more nearly present because she is now a more spiritual being than a creature of flesh and blood and thus more intimate in an invisible bond of love. Although it taxes the mind to accept this paradox—just as it confuses the intelligence to believe that God ascribes the most severe crosses to those whom He especially loves, these truths make it possible to know peace and joy even in the midst of grave sorrows. The truth in letters can offer true solace to the brokenhearted by leading them to the heart of a mystery. Letters often elicit fresh insights, acknowledge hard truths, and illuminate paradoxes that conventional opinions do not penetrate.

In a letter addressed to "My dear Sarah" dated April 3, 1949, C. S. Lewis apologizes for not being able to attend the confirmation of his godchild. However, he offers her some words of wisdom appropriate for the occasion:

> And the bit of advice that comes into my head is this; don't expect (I mean, don't *count on* and don't *demand*) when you are confirmed, or when you make your first Communion, you will have all the *feelings* you would like to have. You may, of course: but you also may not. But don't worry if you don't get them. They aren't what matter. The things that are happening to you are quite real things whether you feel as you would wish or not, just as a meal will do a hungry person good even if he has a cold in the head which will rather spoil the taste. Our Lord will give us the right feelings if He wishes—and then we must say Thank you. If He doesn't, then we must say to ourselves (and Him) that He knows us best. This, by the way, is one of the very few subjects on which I feel I do know something.

Because personal letters are, of course, not intended for publication or large audiences, they often address everyday concerns and practical matters that are overlooked by the popular publications dealing with current events. As Father Schall writes in his chapter "On Essays and Letters" from *On the Unseriousness of Human Affairs*, letters preserve "the particularity of things, without the knowledge of which there is no wisdom." Lewis's letter on confirmation is especially particular—addressed to a special godchild on a memorable occasion— not general or sketchy. The reality of the Christian sacraments where God is intimately present does not necessarily coincide with the experience of new sensations or thrills. It is a subtle topic that requires clarity and elucidation so that the miracle of the sacraments is not confused with the gratifications of physical pleasure. "The Holy Spirit goeth where it listeth, and no man knoweth whence it cometh." The actual reception of the sacraments may or may not provide the feelings of awe, reverence, holiness, and sublimity that often accompany religious mysteries, but that fact does not detract from the actual outpouring of sanctifying grace which the sacraments effect. As in Newman's letter which explains the presence of the absent, Lewis's letter illuminates the hidden life of the soul in which something extraordinary happens when no remarkable signs manifest themselves. Thus letters often evince a simple, natural genius in unraveling complex, delicate matters in a simple, luminous way. So many subtle subjects are best treated in the honest sincerity which letters evoke.

St. Francis de Sales' devotional classic, *Introduction to the Devout Life*—a work that resulted from letters written to Madame de Charmoisy—offers this spiritual insight as a means for attaining the ideal of Christian perfection:

> Real living devotion, Philothea, presupposes the love of God; is in fact that very love, though it has many aspects. In so far as this love adorns the soul and makes us pleasing to God it is called grace; in so far as it empowers us to do good it is called charity; when it is so perfect that it moves us, not merely to do good, but to do good carefully, frequently, and readily, then it is called devotion.

Ostriches never fly, hens fly sometimes but clumsily and not very high, but eagles, doves, and swallows soar upwards swiftly and frequently.

In the same way sinners never fly towards God but travel on the earth seeking only earthly things. Those who are good but not yet devout do fly, but slowly and ungracefully. Those who are devout soar on high to God frequently and readily.

Distinguishing between grace, charity, and devotion and between the sinful, the good, and the devout, de Sales relates the life of the soul to the movement of various birds, illuminating the law of supernatural love by means of a simple analogy from nature. Again letters uncomplicate difficult, abstruse matters with the art of simplicity.

Addressing the spiritual needs and moral questions of an earnest woman seeking to advance in the life of sanctity, de Sales uses common sense and Christian wisdom to make the ideal of a devout life a practical, realistic goal for ordinary Catholics. Personal letters grounded in reality, experience, and truth exercise their wide appeal because they echo with the clarion ring of conviction and carry great weight. They address the real needs of a person and answer pressing questions.

In a letter to the Reverend Dr. Taylor dated April 12, 1784, Dr. Samuel Johnson writes,

Dear Sir,

What can be the reason that I hear nothing from you? I hope nothing disables you from writing. . . . Do not omit giving me the comfort of knowing, that after all my losses I have yet a friend left.

I want every comfort. My life is very solitary and very cheerless. Though it has pleased God wonderfully to deliver me from

the dropsy, I am yet very weak, and have not passed the door since
the 13th of December....

    O! my friend, the approach of death is very dreadful. I am
afraid to think on that which I know I cannot avoid. It is vain to
look round and round for that help which cannot be had. Yet we
hope and hope, and fancy that he who has lived today may live
tomorrow. But let us learn to derive our hope only from God.

    In the mean time, let us be kind to one another. I have no
friend now living but you and Mr. Hector, that was the friend of
my youth. Do not neglect, dear Sir, yours affectionately,

                                       "Sam. Johnson"

In these words Johnson cherishes the letters he receives from
his friends and anticipates the joys and comforts which they
bring. Because Johnson suffers from poor health, the gloom
of loneliness, and the fear of death, letters from friends epitomize light in the midst of darkness. In his anguish Johnson
speaks with unrestrained candor, confessing the anxiety and
trembling of a person approaching his dying days. Striving
to practice the supernatural virtue of hope, Johnson utters
no pious clichés or feigns naïve optimism. Like all humans,
Johnson also must endure the afflictions that attend his own
death and enter the dark night of the soul trusting in God's
mercy. Letters like Johnson's acknowledge the human condition and depict the honest thoughts and heartfelt emotions of
every man contemplating his imminent death. The best letters
render the authentic taste of reality and do not descend to the
level of the superficial, the trite, or the banal.

    These letters, then, embrace all of reality and encompass
the whole range of human experience and thought: Newman
consoling a friend after the loss of his wife, Lewis congratulating

a child upon receiving the sacrament of confirmation, de Sales exhorting a wife on how ordinary people can live a devout life, and Johnson pleading to receive letters from a friend. In short, these most personal letters are agents of grace, God-given sources of strength, comfort, truth, and joy that ennoble, uplift, and inspire. Original, creative, and distinctive, each letter is unrepeatable, having a tone, personality, and sensibility that cannot be duplicated and offering a nourishment to the heart and spirit that no other form of writing equals. As Ann Morrow Lindberg wrote in *Gift from the Sea*, the letter reflects the soul or essence of a person more than his body, physical presence, or appearance which often lead to distractions or preoccupations with the accidental characteristics of clothing and mannerisms. Letters lead us to the center of our lives and to the hearts of others—"the permanent things." They cultivate the value of leisure and contemplation, for one must find time to think, write, and be recollected instead of wasting time watching television or using the internet. Letters by their very nature deal with primary things, important matters, the deepest emotions, and enduring relationships founded in the bonds of love. They accomplish worlds of good, not only by enhancing the quality of daily life with unexpected pleasures and by transmitting human wisdom but also by infusing graciousness and delight into human lives—the reassurance that a person is loved, remembered, cherished, and appreciated in a way that only the personal touch of a letter can convey.

On the other hand, the replacement of personal letters with e-mail correspondence poses many problems. As Clifford Stoll writes in *Silicon Valley: Second Thoughts on the Information Highway* (1995),

E-mail, unlike typed or handwritten letters, discourages reflection. While logged on, it's difficult to compose a message and
then push it aside for review . . . it's too easy to press the send
button. As a result, many letters are sent without thinking of
their consequences.

It's not just a lack of reflection in how we compose our letters, but also in how we read. Instead of contemplating what's
before us, we move on to the next file.

Mr. Stoll offers other criticisms about e-mail: it lacks "the
passion of handwriting," it lacks "style," it cannot deliver "a
perfumed love note," it corrupts the craft of writing, and it robs
correspondence of individuality: "You spend your life devel-
oping your public appearance: it shows in your handwriting,
signature, voice, clothing, and handshake. You leave all this
behind when you send e-mail." Words mean less, and letters via
e-mail reflect a superficiality and triviality that correspond to an
age of hurry intent upon "instant response without reflection,"
a reaction devoid of "reflection or contemplation."

While civilization is transmitted by a society's manners and
morals, it is also perpetuated by its art, literature, and letters.
As internet use and television viewing replace conversation in
homes and as e-mail gains more popularity than letter writing,
the quintessentially human activities where true communication, exchange, and interaction occur suffer. The ersatz replaces
the real, an imaginary virtual reality becomes a substitute for
human experience, communication lacks tact, courtesy, and etiquette, and sophisticated technology spoils the relish of simple
pleasures. Without the restoration of the lost art of personal
letter writing, the noblest sentiments, the wisest advice, and
the most beautiful love letters will not be recorded. The world

will lose some of its most priceless treasures, letters written to beloved people that speak volumes about the graciousness of human hearts. Without the cultivation of this most human of arts, the modern world will fail to acknowledge and record the lofty ideals inspired by such classic letters as the following:

Sarah, my love for you is deathless; it seems to bind me with mighty cables that nothing but Omnipotence could break. . . .

But Oh Sarah! If the dead can come to this earth and flit unseen around those they loved, I shall always be near you; in the gladdest days and in the darkest nights. . . . Always—Always, and if there be a soft breeze upon your cheek, it shall be my breath, as the cool air fans your throbbing temple, it shall be my spirit passing by. Sarah, do not mourn me dead; think I am gone and wait for thee, for we shall meet again. . . .

Letter of Sullivan Ballou to his wife, July 14, 1861

If ever you find yourself environed with difficulties and perplexing circumstances, out of which you are at a loss how to extricate yourself, do what is right, and be assured that that will extricate you the best out of the worst situations. Tho' you cannot see, when you take one step, what will be the next, yet follow truth, justice, and plain dealing, and never fear their leading you out of the labyrinth in the easiest manner possible. The knot which you thought a Gordian one, will untie itself before you.

Letter of Thomas Jefferson to Peter Carr, August 19, 1765

Dad, I wanted to thank you from the bottom of my heart for being my father and for all the sacrifices you have made for me. . . . I am so proud to call you father!! You have taught me so much about life through your example. . . . You have taught me it is more blessed to give than to receive and to strive with all my heart to give back as much as has been given to me. . . .

I am glad you were touched by the wedding—you who only

laugh when something is truly funny and compliment when it is truly deserved. Your comment that our dance was the "quintessence of beauty incarnate" was a compliment that exceeded my expectations.

Dad, I love you so much. I always think of you and Mom when I put on my wedding band. Thanks for bequeathing it to me. I cherish it with all my heart.

Letter of a son to a widowed father, August 31, 2003

No one prizes telephone calls or values e-mail messages in the way the above letters will be cherished and remembered, read and re-read, marveled at and contemplated again and again for generations and generations.

CHAPTER THREE

The Lost Art of Conversation

A S ORDINARY people spend more hours before television screens and computer monitors, as video games and surfing on the internet occupy more and more of a person's leisure time, and as academic life develops more and more online courses and degree programs, the social art of conversation, human interaction, and friendly exchange diminishes. As humans participate more in these unsociable, isolated diversions and less in the hospitable, gregarious experiences of convivial celebration, robust laughter, and animated dialogue, the flow of mirth, wit, and wisdom ebbs. True conversation is not gossip, babble, the mere exchange of information, or argument. Like other purely liberal activities enjoyed for their own sake, conversation encourages the lighthearted, spontaneous play of minds that enjoy the company of others in the round of talk that gracefully jumps from topic to topic in no regular order and moves easily from the comic to the serious, from the ideal to the practical, and from the factual to the anecdotal. Conversation requires no agenda and no Robert's Rules of Order, only the element of mirth and the virtue of civility. When genuine conversation flourishes, wit, banter,

25

and repartee fill the air; ideas are exchanged and clarified; and wisdom and prudence appear. Conversation expands the heart, nourishes the mind, and refreshes the spirit, for man by nature is a social (political) animal who desires to know. While computer highways and information systems disseminate information and news, they do not communicate the common sense, perennial wisdom, and self-knowledge that the art of conversation cultivates.

In his famous biography *The Life of Samuel Johnson*, James Boswell acknowledges the hallmark of his book: his assiduity "to preserve his [Johnson's] conversation in an authentick [sic] and lively manner" and his scrupulosity "by which so many conversations were recorded." Renowned for his immense learning, remarkable wisdom, witty conversation, and honest talk, Dr. Johnson illuminates the meaning of the art of conversation. His many remarks on the topic indicate a hierarchy of various degrees of conversation ranging from pleasant talk to intellectual invigoration. First, simple conversation promotes charity, good will, and friendship and does not demand scintillating wit or learned sophistication: "That is the happiest conversation where there is no competition, no vanity, but a calm quiet interchange of sentiments," Johnson remarks. When Boswell once complained about the absence of stimulating conversation at a dinner which provided a sumptuous banquet, he asked "Why then meet at table?" Johnson explained that good conversation did not demand intellectual substance: "Why, to eat and drink together, and to promote kindness." Boswell also records another comment of Johnson that highlights the social, civilizing dimension of conversation—not its educational content: "The happiest conversation is that of which nothing is distinctly remembered but a general effect of pleasing impression."

Second, good conversation invites playfulness and cultivates mirth and laughter. In the spirit of pure fun Johnson easily assumed the role of "the greatest sophist" and the most subtle devil's advocate, and his quick wit was unparalleled, for Boswell recalls the famous actor David Garrick's remark: "Rabelais and all other wits are nothing compared with him. You may be diverted by them; but Johnson gives you a forcible hug, and shakes laughter out of you, whether you will or no." Boswell's lifelong friendship with Johnson provided copious examples of the great sage's fun-loving good nature: "He frequently indulged himself in colloquial pleasantry; and the heartiest merriment was often enjoyed in his company."

Third, civil conversation enlarges the mind and develops the power of thinking in the spirit of friendly competition. Notorious for his passion for victory in argument ("sometimes too desirous of triumph in colloquial contest"), Johnson enjoyed the sharpening of his mental acumen that honest discussion and lively debate provoked. Boswell elaborates: "He had, however, all his life habituated himself to consider conversation as a trial of intellectual vigor and skill." Especially in his exchanges with Edmund Burke, the eminent statesman, Johnson exercised the power of his mind to the utmost. As Boswell recalls, "Mr. Burke having been mentioned, he said, 'That fellow calls forth all my powers. Were I to see Burke now, it would kill me.' So much was he accustomed to consider conversation as a contest, and such was his notion of Burke as an opponent." Thus the art of conversation cultivates charitable fellowship, elicits playful wit and innocent laughter, and broadens the mind.

Johnson, the epitome of the kindness, mirth, and learning that conversation evokes, also distinguishes between genuine and counterfeit conversation, and he recognizes the bad manners that spoil the enjoyment of true conversation. He warned that idle curiosity and officious meddlesomeness ("questioning") do not nourish the spirit of friendly conversation: "Questioning is not the mode of conversation among gentlemen. It is assuming a superiority, and it is particularly wrong to question a man concerning himself." Johnson also objected to exhibitionism in conversation, a type of self-glorification that boasted of notorious deeds: "A man should be careful never to tell tales of himself to his own disadvantage. People may be amused and laugh at the time, but they will be remembered and brought out against him upon some subsequent occasion."

Likewise, it is poor manners to confine the subject of conversation to one topic and exclude the general interests of the many. Boswell writes, "Being irritated by hearing a gentleman ask Mr. Levett a variety of questions concerning him [Johnson], when he was sitting by, he broke out, 'Sir, you have but two topics, yourself and me. I am sick of both.'" Johnson, a "clubbable" man always eager to engage in conversation, commended this quality in others and considered taciturnity a form of incivility. The pleasure which Dr. Brocklesby's company afforded him consisted in his "never-failing source of conversation" based on his "reading, and knowledge of life, and good spirits," and Johnson delighted in Mr. Edwards, an old acquaintance from college, even though his friend lacked the breadth of learning and knowledge of life as a whole: "Why, yes, Sir. Here is a man who has passed through life without experience: yet I would rather have him with me than a more sensible man who will not talk readily. This man is willing to say what he has to say." Boswell notes that Johnson, even in a state of illness, "had none of that unsocial shyness which we commonly see in people afflicted with sickness. He did not hide his head from the world, in solitary abstraction; he did not deny himself the visits of his friends and acquaintances; but at all times . . . was ready for conversation as in his best days." Johnson also judged it bad manners to host an occasion for conversation and friendship and neglect the serving of refreshments, objecting "it will never do, Sir. There is nothing served there, neither tea, nor coffee, nor lemonade, nor any thing whatever; and depend upon it, Sir, a man does not love to go to a place from whence he comes out exactly as he came in." In short, the civility required for occasions of conversation demands tact, moderation, humility, conviviality, and magnanimity—the ability to avoid unpleasant topics, boastful exaggeration, narrow interests, and apathetic indifference. According to Boswell, Johnson himself exemplified this ideal: "On the contrary, the truth is, that by much the greatest part of the time he was civil, obliging, polite in the true sense of the word; so much so, that many gentlemen, who were long acquainted with him, never received, or even heard a strong expression from him."

This practice of civil conversation has also gone the way of the lost arts of letter writing, hospitality, and the enjoyment of people as perennial sources of great joy. As television and film viewing and video games and internet occupy more time and leisure, solitary, silent activities replace sociable, hospitable occasions. The particular virtues that the art of conversation instills—the ability to listen, the willingness to please, the practice of self-forgetfulness, the habit of tact, the exploration of another's mind, and the desire to enlarge one's world—all suffer a lack of development. Emotional and mental impoverishment follows, and the habit of graciousness and delicacy receives less cultivation. If the arts of conversation are not learned and practiced, human beings and their personal stories evoke no interest, pleasing one's self assumes greater importance than tending to others, people are not appreciated for their intrinsic goodness and unique gifts, proper respect and thoughtful consideration are neglected, opportunities for learning and broadening one's experience are frustrated, and the chance to acquire the wisdom and prudence of others is foiled. Thus the virtual reality of chat rooms, on-line instruction, and talk show programs gives the illusion of the exchange and interaction of dialogue, but these imitations do not represent the reality of actual conversation that Boswell's biography captures.

For Johnson conversation is not only enjoyable sociability and an expression of thoughtful kindness but also an intellectual skill that sharpens the mind—the peak of the hierarchy of the many levels of conversation. As he explained to Boswell,

> There must, in the first place, be knowledge, there must be materials; in the second place, there must be a command of words; in the third place, there must be imagination, to place things in such views as they are not commonly seen in; and in the fourth place, there must be presence of mind, and the resolution that is not to be overcome with failures.

In short, nothing can come from nothing. A well-stocked mind "replete with images," as Johnson said of Imlac's intelligence in his short novel *Rasselas*, possesses "materials," the richest storehouse for the pleasures of conversation. Imlac, the sage in Johnson's novel—conversant with the world of commerce, navigation, and literature—has traveled widely and acquired the knowledge of men and manners that informs his capacious mind. Because he possesses a mind "replete with images"—knowledge from experience, books, and travel—he escapes the "perpetual vacancy" that robs the spirit of the liveliness of conversation. Imlac also employs "imagination" in his conversation, the ability to grasp old truths in original ways instead of as tired platitudes. When the young prince Rasselas asks Imlac about the reason for the Egyptian pyramids, enormous monuments which serve no great practical purpose in proportion to their cost and labor, Imlac offers this unexpected but revealing answer: "He that has built for use, till use is supplied, must begin to build for vanity, and extend his plan to the utmost power of human performance, that he may not be soon reduced to form another wish. . . . I consider this mighty structure as a monument of the insufficiency of human enjoyments." This fresh insight illustrates Johnson's meaning of imagination in conversation as the ability "to place things in such views as they are not commonly seen in." Lastly, Imlac exemplifies "the presence of mind" or equanimity that good conversation requires when he explains the human condition to Rasselas as a constant struggle between reason and fancy: "There is no man whose imagination does not sometimes prevail over his reason. . . . No man will be found in whose mind airy notions do not sometimes tyrannize, and force him to hope or fear beyond the limits of sober probability." The astronomer, the scientist whose solitary life in the observatory has deprived him of the pleasures and sobriety of conversation, suffers from a "dangerous prevalence of the imagination" that leads to fantasizing and daydreaming, and he has lost all presence of mind which the art of conversation develops. He believes that he controls the weather.

Thus the virtue of conversation not only develops the mind and increases knowledge, making a person "replete with images," an essential ingredient of human happiness, but also cures nonsense and flights of fancy that assume the form of utopian ideas and unrealistic theories. In his conversation Johnson on many occasions exposed what he called "cant," affectations and pretensions which contradicted common sense. In one instance Boswell claimed that David Hume and Samuel Foote boasted that they did not fear death. Johnson replied, "It is not true, Sir. Hold a pistol to Foote's breast, or to Hume's breast, and threaten to kill them, and you'll see how they behave." Johnson then asked Boswell if he would believe that anyone putting his finger in a flame felt no pain. On another occasion Boswell asked Johnson if he would eat his dinner if a friend were apprehended for a crime and hanged, implying that close associates claimed they would fast. Again Johnson's rejoinder ridicules this sentimentality: "Yes, Sir; and eat it as if he were eating it with me. Why there's Baretti, who is to be tried for his life tomorrow, friends have risen up for him on every side; yet if he should be hanged, none of them would eat a slice of plum-pudding the less." In another example when Boswell asserted that a life in public affairs would "vex" him extremely if Parliament acted contrary to his wishes, Johnson replied, "That's cant, Sir. It would not vex you more in the house, than in the gallery. Public affairs vex no man," and he concluded, "My dear friend, clear your mind of cant."

Likewise, Johnson advised Boswell not to "cant" on behalf of the cult of the noble savage, the idea of primitivism popularized by Rousseau that equated the ideal of happiness with the desire to "return to nature" and learn from the noble Indian: "Do not allow yourself, Sir, to be imposed upon by such gross absurdity. If a bull could speak, he might as well explain—'Here am I with this cow and this grass; what being can enjoy greater felicity?'" Thus good conversation at its best restores common sense and cures folly, dispelling exaggerations, clichés, and silly ideas by its sobriety. Like the medicine of laughter that cures star-gazing abstract philosophers by bringing them down to earth as they fall in a ditch, good conversation clears the mind of cant and stops a person from thinking foolishly.

When virtual classrooms and on-line "Blackboard" programs replace actual oral human communication, the qualities and benefits of good conversation that Johnson relishes are absent from learning. An essential tool of education— dialogue—has disappeared. The pure enjoyment of a person's personality is never discovered, and the amiability, charm, or mirth in the quality of a person's voice is lost. One of life's exquisite pleasures has been omitted. When family members watch television during their meals and fail to interact in the normal exchanges of conversation about the day's happenings, sociability and friendship decline. The joy of discovering and knowing a person's family history and the ethnic, religious heritage of a person's traditions and roots remains unknown. As individuals consume time on the internet and spend their hours playing computer games and watching films as their primary sources of recreation, the virtues of civility and graciousness are not habitually practiced. Fun is no longer spending time with the people who are loved and befriended but an isolated, individualistic activity that never contributes to the happiness of others. The verbal arts of wit, repartee, storytelling, and joking become obsolete without the normal, natural experience of human conversation on a myriad of subjects. As gravity replaces lightheartedness and dullness supplants the comic muse, humans lose their sense of mirth and their ability to be a child. Without the enjoyment of conversation as a normative means of learning, the pursuit of learning grows ever more impersonal and mechanical. All the gifts of language that Johnson excelled in—wit, playfulness, repartee irony, satire—reflect a highly developed sense of humor that follows from a life rich in conversation. The most genuine sources of laughter flow from lively conversation as Boswell's *Life of Johnson* illustrates in his praise of "the wonderful dexterity and readiness of Johnson's wit." In one of the spontaneous outbursts of this wit, Johnson remarked, "Sir, it is no matter what you teach them [children] first, any more than what leg you shall put into your breeches first. Sir, you may stand disputing which is best to put in first, but in the meantime your breech is bare." As Leon Kass, M.D., writes in *The Hungry Soul* (1994), the appreciation of friendship and love in the midst of sharing a meal and enjoying the conversation of others naturally leads to "the meeting and cherishing of souls," a movement "through playful conversation and wit in the direction of the pursuit of wisdom." In this atmosphere of the enjoyable companionship of friends and family, "one person's speech turns another's mind around" as conversation "enables us to taste, indeed to savor, the souls of our fellow diners" and to discover "that wonderful side of the soul at play, when it is unselfconsciously and immediately being its open, companionable, and responsive self." That is, in the true art of conversation one discovers that others are indeed more "real" than one imagined as Chesterton would say. This is the unique virtue of Boswell's famous biography, a portrait of a "literary Colossus," a heroic man, an eminent moralist, a "clubbable" man renowned for his capacity for great friendships, and the most enjoyable conversationalist of his time who inspired his friends to say, "Let us go to the next best:— there is nobody; no man can put you in mind of Johnson." Without the habit of conversation in homes, schools, and social occasions, the memorable reality of people, the sheer enjoyment of the play of speech, the liveliness of the truth, and the medicine of common sense leave the realm of ordinary experience and become the vestiges of an ancient past, and the whole quality of life becomes reduced to the banal and the pathetic.

CHAPTER 4

The Lost Art of Enjoying People

"NO MAN can live without pleasure," St. Thomas Aquinas wrote, for human beings are created for happiness and beatitude. The pleasures appropriate for human beings of course are rational pleasures that civilized humans enjoy in accordance with moral laws. The pleasures of eating and drinking, for example, must never degenerate into the sin of gluttony or drunkenness. Likewise, the enjoyment of learning must never deteriorate into pride or curiosity, and the delight of chaste, marital love is not to be confused with the pleasure of lust. In their natural desire for pleasure humans enjoy the whole gamut of sources of happiness from the pleasures of the five senses to the entertainment of the arts to the possession of worldly things. Eating in restaurants, hearing classical music, viewing movies and plays, traveling to foreign countries, watching professional sports, swimming on the beaches of Hawaii, and reading great literature all represent the rational, human pleasures that civilized people savor. In Western societies where materialism and consumerism run riot, expensive gifts, modern conveniences, and new technologies multiply the sources of pleasure to include new cars, video games, surfing on the internet, e-mail, cable television, and cell phones. A person is never at a loss on how to be amused or diverted whether at home, in the car, at the mall, or in the city. But in this pursuit of pleasure and entertainment, the greatest source of happiness—the enjoyment of persons—is downplayed and underestimated. The gift for enjoying people has become a lost art.

Of course people still socialize, entertain guests, and spend the holidays with friends and family, but more time is spent viewing sports on television, watching films at home, playing video games, and using the internet than enjoying the company of friends, hosting occasions of hospitality, and delighting in good conversation. The decline in population in Western Europe and America is one symptom of this loss of the enjoyment of people, of the delight in children. In a culture in which a society is not replacing itself, the enjoyment of children as one of life's greatest sources of happiness holds no privileged place in the hierarchy of pleasures. Somehow there is no time or energy in the affluent West to found large families, but there is ample time for education, for a career, for travel, and for self-improvement. The increase in divorce and the rise of the promiscuous relationships of cohabitation also reflect the failure of humans to value others enough to love, cherish, and rejoice in them for a lifetime. The novelty of pleasure a person offers seems only short-term or minimal. The trend in America to institutionalize or isolate the elderly is another manifestation of this inability to appreciate the joy of people. Like cheap products, used cars, or temporary fashions, people appear as ephemeral pleasures or replaceable items—not an investment for a lifetime or an eternity. Keats said, "A thing of beauty is a joy forever," but humans are no longer considered as creatures of infinite goodness or eternal happiness. The depreciation of the sacredness of life manifested in the legalization of abortion and euthanasia also cheapens the value of persons as sources of endless joy.

Because persons are rational, social, and spiritual beings, they possess depths and riches— inexhaustible fountains of goodness, love, joy, and mirth that overflow into sources of happiness for many others. A child is a joy for a brother or sister, a gift to parents, a blessing to grandparents, a delight to friends, a lover to a spouse, and life's greatest benefactor to his or her own children. To enjoy people is to marvel at their uniqueness and remarkable individuality. As Gerard Manley Hopkins wrote in "Comments on the Spiritual Exercises of St. Ignatius Loyola," "I find myself both as man and as myself something most determined and distinctive, at pitch, more distinctive and higher pitched than anything else I see." He compares his "selfbeing" and "taste of myself" to spices and herbs, "more distinctive than the taste of ale or alum, more distinctive than the smell of walnutleaf or camphor." Just as seasonings and spices give savor and aroma to enhance the taste of food, human beings lend flavor and color to daily experience and transform the atmosphere of a place or the quality of a day. One person missing from the family table or absent at a special occasion alters the entire tone of the event. People mourn their loved ones who have died, lament their absence because of long distance, and yearn for the company and presence of those they love because they are unrepeatable and irreplaceable in their individuality. As the young boy Diamond remarks in George MacDonald's *At the Back of the North Wind*, "Somehow when once you've looked into anybody's eyes, right deep down into them, I mean, nobody will do for that one anymore. Nobody, ever so beautiful or good, will make up for that one going out of sight." As the inscription on Jane Austen's tombstone in Winchester Cathedral reads, "The benevolence of her heart, the sweetness of her temperament, the extraordinary endowments of her mind, obtained the regard of all who knew her. . . . Their grief is in proportion to their affection; they know their loss to be irreparable. . . ." Thus, despite Sartre's infamous remark that "hell is other people," humans are inexhaustible joys for ever and touch many lives.

The spiritual depths in human nature foster relationships of intimacy, oneness, and communion in the bonds of love and friendship, one of life's greatest pleasures. In the union of marriage the two become one in body and soul; in the oneness of friendship the friend becomes an alter ego, an other self; in the closeness of family relationships brothers and sisters develop, to use Hopkins' phrase from his poem "Brothers," "love-laced hearts" intricately and delicately threaded by their shared history and common memories:

> How lovely the elder brother's
> Life all laced in the other's,
> Love-laced!

In these intimate ties formed by a lifetime of shared memories and experiences, the joys of one are experienced by the other, and the sorrows of one are felt by the other: in these close relationships joys are doubled and sorrows are divided by half. Because of man's godlike nature and the spiritual nature of love, the heart expands, love grows, and a person cherishes a loving spouse, beloved children, devoted parents, and loyal friends more and more with each passing year. John Donne expresses this richness of a human relationship in his poem "Lovers Infiniteness":

Thou canst not every day give me thy heart,
If thou gavest it, then thou never gavest it:
Loves riddles are, that though thy heart depart,
It stayes at home, and thou with losing savest it.

In his poem "Loves Growth," Donne, in the style of metaphysical wit, compares this infinite growth of love to the concentric circles in a body of water and to princes increasing taxes in times of war which they never rescind in times of peace. These depths of goodness in persons resemble the miraculous pitcher in Hawthorne's story from *A Wonder Book*, a tale about the boundless hospitality of Baucis and Philemon to all strangers. In gratitude for the generous welcome they receive from the elderly couple, the travelers (Greek gods in disguise) reward their hosts with a miraculous pitcher that never lacks a supply of milk. Resembling the kind hearts of Baucis and Philemon which never stop giving, the pitcher continues to fill milk cups with its infinite sources of milk. In the *Confessions* St. Augustine also marvels at the abundance of love and care he received from his mother and his nurse: "Their feelings were so ordered that they wanted to give me something of that abundance which they received from you." In other words, the pleasure that loving people provide is bountiful and inexhaustible—not a short-lived consumer item.

Human beings also are great sources of comedy and laughter. The antics of children reveling in innocent play, the banter between husband and wife in the mirth of marriage, and old men joking and reminiscing all evoke the pleasure of laughter. Whether it is the bawdy story of Chaucer's "The Miller's Tale" when clever Nicholas the scholar is "branded in the toute" (scorched on the buttocks), the adventure of Don Quixote confronting the windmills and calling them giants, or the rude mechanicals in Shakespeare's *A Midsummer Night's Dream* apologizing to the women that the lion in their play of *Pyramus and Thisbe* is not really a lion but Snug the joiner, the comic spirit evokes irrepressible laughter at the folly of ridiculous man. For example, lest the women be offended by the violence of a lion on stage, Bottom in Shakespeare's play proposes by way of explanation a prologue: "I would entreat you—not to fear, not to tremble. My life for yours. If you think I come hither as a lion, it were pity of my life. No, I am no such thing. I am a man as other men are." In *Life on the Mississippi* Mark Twain recounts the tale of the pilot who unwittingly gives the wheel for five minutes to a sleepwalker and goes downstairs for coffee. When asked who is at the helm, the pilot says "X," only to learn that the man at the wheel is a notorious sleepwalker. Rushing upstairs and discovering that no one is at the helm while the steamboat is exactly on course, the pilot jokes, "You just ought to have seen him take this boat through Helena crossing. I never saw anything so gaudy before. And if he can do such gold-leaf, kid-glove, diamond-breastpin piloting when he is sound asleep, what *couldn't* he do if he was dead!" The wealth of comic literature testifies that by man by nature is *homo ludens* (a playful being), and the great comic writers like Chaucer, Shakespeare, Cervantes, and Twain illustrate the sheer delight that risible humans afford to one another. As Henry Fielding, another renowned comic novelist, wrote, "And there is one reason why a comic writer should of all others be the least excused for deviating from nature," namely, "life everywhere furnishes an accurate observer with the ridiculous."

Along with the pleasure of love, friendship, and laughter that humans offer to one another, the art of enjoying people also includes the pleasure of conversation. Boswell's biography of Samuel Johnson, the eminent eighteenth century man of letters, abounds in the copious wit and wisdom of one of the most accomplished conversationalists of all time. For example, when Boswell remarks that he would be "vexed" if he were a member of the House of Parliament and political affairs went contrary to his wishes, Johnson responds, "That's cant, sir. It would not vex you more in the house, than in the gallery: publick affairs vex no man." Puzzled that Johnson is not seriously disturbed about "the turbulent reign" of the monarch and the "absurd vote of the House of Commons," Boswell's exaggerated complaint appears silly after Johnson's rejoinder: "Sir, I have never slept an hour less, nor eat an ounce less meat. I would have knocked the dogs on the head, to be sure; but I was not *vexed*. . . . You may *talk* in this manner; it is a mode of talking in Society: but don't *think* foolishly." In *Life on the Mississippi* Mark Twain relishes his days as a cub pilot on the river because of hearing the conversation of colorful shipmates shouting orders, discharging them "like a blast of lightning" instead of saying "please":

> Lively, now! What're you about! Snatch it! *Snatch* it! There! There! Aft again! Aft again! Don't you hear me? Dash it to dash! Are you going to *sleep* over it? 'Vast heaving. 'Vast heaving, I tell you! . . .

Where're you going with that barrel! *For'ard* with it 'fore I make
you swallow it. . . .

Savoring the tang and admiring the verve of this wild,
homespun eloquence, Twain writes, "I wished I could talk
like that." In *Don Quixote* when the knight-errant addresses
the landlady of the inn with elegant courtesy, they marvel at
the poetry of his language: "I shall keep engraved for all time
in my memory the service you have done me. . . . Would to
high heaven that Love had not enthralled me and subjected me
to his laws and to the eyes of the beautiful Dulcinea . . . else
would the eyes of this beauteous damsel here bereave me of my
freedom." When Sancho Panza, on the other hand, minces no
words in his sharp denunciation of doctors who deprive him of
his favorite foods, his conversation elicits peals of laughter: "I'll
so rib-roast and belabour all the physic-mongers in the island
that not one of them will be left—I mean of those like yourself
whom I know to be ignorant quacks. . . ." In these famous
samples of conversation—the scintillating wit of Johnson, the
animated spontaneity of the shipmate, the poetic prose of Don
Quixote, and the blunt honesty of Sancho Panza—the listener
experiences the spark of truth, the flamboyance of language,
the charm of compliments, and the brevity of wit. Like clothing, the pleasure of conversation offers many styles and serves
many purposes from illuminating the truth to moving the will
to melting the heart to exposing nonsense.

Because persons also possess a wealth of information and
storehouses of counsel, they offer the pleasure of learning and
transmit the wisdom of the past and the knowledge of experience. Different from formal education and bookish learning,

this familiar relationship in which child learns from parent, apprentice learns from master, and "old birds teach young birds how to fly," to use C. S. Lewis's term from *The Abolition of Man*, disseminates knowledge in the most personal of ways: *cor ad cor loquitur* (heart speaks to heart). Knowledge lives in human beings, not in libraries or bookstores. In the Christian faith the truth is a person, the *Logos*, the Word made Flesh. In the Book of Proverbs wisdom is a woman ("Be busy to seek her"), and in classical philosophy wisdom is Lady Philosophy. In Boethius's *Consolation of Philosophy*, Boethius, having forgotten all the wisdom he acquired from his formal study of philosophy in the schools, lies in prison in a state of melancholy, self-pity, and despair. Only when Lady Philosophy appears in the form of a beautiful woman with "eyes burning and keen" and with "a vivid color and undiminished vigour" to administer the medicine of wisdom does Boethius regain his equanimity and self-possession. In Dante's *Divine Comedy* Dante the pilgrim learns about the laws of God's justice and mercy in Purgatory from his guide Virgil and about the mysteries of the law of human and heavenly love from his mentor Beatrice:

> My eyes once more had sought my lady's face
> And with my mind, were fixed on her, the while
> All other thoughts to her had yielded place.

In his apprenticeship as a cub pilot on the Mississippi, Mark Twain learned from his master, Mr. Bixby, that a captain must read all 1,200 miles of the river "as if it were a book" and memorize "all the million trifling variations of shape in the banks of this interminable river" as well as he knew the shape of the front hall at home in the dark. Through wise, experienced, and learned people, one experiences the joys of learning and the love of wisdom. Boethius learns from Lady Philosophy that law, not chance—God's Divine Providence, not fickle fortune—rules the world. Dante learns from Beatrice that a spiritual good (love)—unlike material possessions (money) which diminish when shared—always increases when given. Mark Twain learns from Mr. Bixby that "you've got to know the shape of the river perfectly. It is all there is left to steer by on a very dark night." All these treasures of knowledge—human wisdom, the law of love, practical skill—are transmitted by persons talking to persons in the lively exchange of conversation and dialogue.

If human beings, then, are sheer delight because of their infinite variety, overflowing fountains of joy, love, and goodness because of their spiritual depths, and bountiful sources of laughter, conversation, and wisdom because of their playful, rational, and social nature, why are people not fully appreciated as life's greatest source of true pleasure? Why has a love of things surpassed the enjoyment of people, and why have the more temporal pursuits of gratification—travel, education, career, health—replaced the more eternal sources of happiness? In a consumerist society one is accustomed to purchasing pleasure, receiving instant gratification, and living in comfortable ease. However, the enjoyment of persons is an art, and like all arts (*ars longa, vita brevis*—art is long, life is brief), it requires time, effort, practice, patience, and commitment. It takes an effort to know a person, initiate a conversation, cultivate a friendship, conduct a courtship, or receive guests with hospitality. The pleasure of a child demands constant care, diligent teaching, and habitual training in manners and morals. The joy of a marriage tests both husband and wife to give, love, and sacrifice more and more in the course of a whole lifetime—to carry crosses, to honor vows "till death do us part," and to be generous and forgiving. The pleasure of friendship involves visits, letters, invitations, and communication. Unlike fast consumerist purchases with a credit card, these arts require a lifetime of cultivation for perfection.

For example, in Jane Austen's *Pride and Prejudice*, Darcy frustrates his courtship with Elizabeth Bennet because he would not deign to dance with her at a ball and could not be bothered to engage in civil conversation. Elizabeth rejects Darcy's first marriage proposal because he failed to woo her properly and gain her respect and admiration. Darcy failed to take the time and make the effort that all true romance requires. Later in the novel when Darcy proposes a second time—after he has learned the art of appreciating people—Elizabeth accepts his offer because he demonstrates genuine courtesy, expresses warm cordiality, and reveals real tokens of sincere love. Their romance involved many tests and requirements and developed slowly and gradually in the course of time as Darcy learned to modify his prideful behavior and Elizabeth required time to discover Darcy's true noble character. Dr. Samuel Johnson, renowned for his many lifelong, loyal friendships with people of all ages and from all the ranks of life, explained the art of friendship: "If a man does not make new acquaintance as he advances through life, he will soon find himself alone. A man, sir, should keep his friendship in constant repair. On Mondays, "clean shirt day," Johnson found the time, exerted the effort, and extended himself to cultivate his many friendships with weekly visits. Louisa May Alcott's *Little Men* compares the work of parents and teachers educating children to tending a garden with "the greatest skill and care," the art of tender love, constant nurture, and eternal vigilance to ensure the rich harvest of seeing ordinary boys mature into civilized, mature men:" Father and Mother Bhaer's crop was of a different sort, and not so easily described; but they were satisfied with it, felt that their summer work had prospered well, and by and by had a harvest that made them very happy." The art of enjoying people, then, obliges persons to give attention, to provide care, to find time, to build friendships, to nurture love, and to delight in human beings for their own sake. These arts resemble the slow, time-consuming natural process of cultivating, sowing, weeding, and reaping and do not happen by magic. *Ars longa.*

However, in the Western societies of the twenty-first century—the culture of easy divorce, casual cohabitation, physician-assisted suicide, and abortion on demand—comfort and convenience govern humans rather than the acquired arts of living. Instead of expending effort in honoring vows, in raising children, in learning to grow in marital love, in exercising patience with the elderly, the mentality in Huxley's *Brave New World* prevails: "Ending is better than mending." As a character in the novel remarks, "Fine to think we can go on being socially useful even after we're dead. Make plants grow." Thus people are dispensable and replaceable, and they are viewed in utilitarian terms rather than in terms of their intrinsic worth. Whereas marriage obliges a man and woman to honor each other, courtship requires a man to respect a woman, the care of the elderly esteems their venerability, and the nurture of children values their preciousness, the modern secular view of persons regards them as obsolescent things. The contraceptive mentality, Pope Paul VI explained in *Humanae Vitae*, encourages a husband to regard his wife as an object, "a mere instrument of selfish pleasure, and no longer as his respected and beloved companion." The techniques of artificial reproduction, Pope John Paul II explains in *Evangelium Vitae*, classify embryos not used in implantation as " 'biological material' to be freely disposed of." Thus when human beings are categorized as convenient things, disposable parts, obsolete items, and means to an end, they are judged, according to John Paul II, by "the criterion of efficiency, functionality, and usefulness"—not for what human beings "are" but for what they possess, produce, or do. Humans, then, are not enjoyed for their own sake but as a means to an end—as things to be manipulated, experimented upon, and exploited.

The art of enjoying people, however, views them as ends in themselves, as gifts to appreciate, and as persons who are inherently lovable for their own sake. The favor of their company and presence, a delight in their special, unrepeatable individuality, and the gladness of mirth which good people radiate, enrich human life with priceless treasure.

George Macdonald's famous poem in his book *At the Back of the North Wind* depicts the absolute joy that a child brings into the world:

Where did you come from, baby dear?
Out of the everywhere into the here.
Where did you get your eyes so blue?
Out of the sky as I came through.
What makes the light in them sparkle and spin?
Some of the starry spikes left in.

In Shakespeare's *The Tempest* Miranda marvels not only at the ideal of manhood that Ferdinand personifies but also at the abundant variety of human nature she beholds for the first time:

> O, wonder!
> How many goodly creatures are there here!
> How beauteous mankind is! Oh, brave new world,
> That has such people in't!

In Boswell's *Life of Johnson* the death of the eminent man of letters renowned for his warm friendship, immense learning, and remarkable wisdom inspired these words of praise: "He has made a chasm, which not only nothing can fill up, but which nothing has a tendency to fill up. Johnson is dead. Let us go to the next best:—there is nobody; no man can be said to put you in mind of Johnson." In all these examples the people are cherished, valued, and loved for their own sake, as ends in themselves, simply because they "are."

Once the pleasure of things replaces the enjoyment of people, the entire quality of a civilization suffers. People become secondary in a person's life, and all the virtues that govern human relationships—justice, friendship, charity, mercy, courtesy—lose their significance. If people do not desire children, if friendship no longer constitutes "the wine of life," if families do not host occasions of hospitality, and if people find more happiness in finite worldly things than in eternal human treasure, then humans lose their vision of life's meaning and purpose. If human laws encourage or legalize practices (divorce, same-sex marriage, abortion, euthanasia) that violate the primary and quintessential human relationships between man and woman, between parents and children, and between the old and the young, then people witness the dehumanization that C. S. Lewis called "the abolition of man" in his book by that title. Man is reduced from God's work of art as a person created in His image who inspires Miranda's "O, wonder," to what Lewis calls "a trousered ape," "the urban blockhead," or "a man without a chest."

CHAPTER FIVE

The Art of Pleasing

A FATHER or mother never finds time to cultivate friendships or create fun for the children. A husband always finds time for his favorite pastimes but never does favors for his wife. A wife goes shopping for groceries and prepares meals only to gratify her sense of taste and ignores the preferences of other members of the family. Adult children never remember the birthdays or anniversaries of their parents and even neglect to write simple thank you notes. People are invited as guests for many festive occasions or dinner parties but do not attend, or they never host celebrations in their own home or extend hospitality to others. In each of these examples a person does not exert the effort to please another person by performing a simple gesture of thoughtfulness. These careless omissions affect the entire quality of social life within families and also among friends and spoil many occasions of happiness

One of the marks of refinement, civility, and graciousness is the willingness to bring joy into human lives by gratuitous acts of special kindness that respect the wishes or feelings of others—the art of pleasing. The peacefulness of family life, the enjoyment of friendships, and the harmony of marriage rest

upon this art, a skill that attunes persons to the particular preferences and individual sensibilities of others' personalities. This
virtue requires humility and the desire to serve others rather
than willfully insisting on one's own way or thinking exclusively
of one's own pleasure or convenience. These matters of pleasing
others and sensitivity to others' likes and dislikes do not address
great moral issues of good or evil or momentous existential
decisions but attend to the social graces of manners.

In *By Love Refined* Alice von Hildebrand writes of a wife's
simple request for her husband not to place a bar of soap in a
dish of water—certainly not a matter of high importance in
the scale of priorities. Of the many obligations in the course
of a person's daily duties, remembering not to put the soap
in the water does not assume first place in the daily round of
responsibilities. Yet a husband's wish to please his wife and
remember her request proves his love and touches her heart:
the pure desire to please the beloved offers sure evidence of real
love. This considerate responsiveness and immediate fulfillment
of a request produce greater happiness and appreciation than
expected and enhance the entire quality of daily life. The art of
pleasing inspires a grateful heart and moves a person to return
favors and cherish someone's fond affection.

The refusal to practice the art of pleasing severs human
relationships and prevents the growth of love and devotion
between parents and children, between husbands and wives,
and between friends. If happiness is the sum of little things, the
failure to practice the art of pleasing deprives all relationships
of exquisite pleasures. In Shakespeare's *King Lear* the elderly
king bestows his rich inheritance and royal power to his two
elder daughters Goneril and Regan upon the condition that

he and his attendants receive hospitality in their visits to the daughters' castles. Irritated at their father's insistence that they host both king and a hundred retainers, Goneril and Regan refuse to please. Regan protests: "what, fifty followers?/ Is it not well? What should you need of more/ . . . 'Tis hard, almost impossible." Goneril also insists on her own way and finds her father's request unreasonable: "What need you five and twenty, ten, or five,/ To follow in a house where twice so many/ Have a command to tend you?" Lear's daughters will not accommodate their father, disrespecting his kingship and dishonoring their promise—a breach that breaks his fatherly heart and alienates him from his children.

Wounded and heartbroken by his daughters' cruel ingratitude, Lear laments, "I gave you all" and vents his righteous anger:

> Oh, reason not the need. Our basest beggars
> Are in the poorest thing superfluous.
> Allow not nature more than nature needs,
> Man's life's as cheap as beast's. Thou art a lady.
> If only to go warm were gorgeous,
> Why, nature needs not what thou gorgeous wear'st,
> Which scarcely keeps thee warm. (II. iv. 268-273)

Lear's passionate indignation recalls the meaning of human dignity and the purpose of pleasing others. The art of pleasing is not a question of necessity or utility but a matter of refinement and respect. Pleasing a father just for the sake of delighting him is no more necessary than wearing attractive clothing or adorning the human body for the sake of beauty. The art of pleasing is an "extra," something in addition that transcends the obligations of justice—a gratuity that acknowledges the specialness of the person. The careless neglect of Goneril and Regan in this domestic matter of honoring their father's legitimate wishes destroys the filial bond of children and father and leads to the grave injustices that follow in Shakespeare's tragedy. The oneness of the family bond and the harmony between the generations suffer when the art of pleasing becomes a lost art or empty protocol.

In Jane Austen's *Pride and Prejudice* the aristocratic, prideful Darcy refuses to be obliging and pleasing at a ball. Neglecting the amenities of mixing and mingling with the guests, of initiating and conducting civil conversation, and dancing with the young ladies who need partners, Darcy leaves a bad impression and acts like a boor. Austen writes, ". . . his manners gave a disgust which turned the tide of his popularity; for he was discovered to be proud, to be above his company, and above being pleased." Too haughty to forget himself and please others, Darcy especially offends Elizabeth Bennet, an elegant, attractive woman who piques his romantic interest. However, no romance happens under the circumstances because he failed in the art of pleasing both the young ladies and their parents: "He was the proudest, most disagreeable man in the world, and every body hoped that he would never come there again." Darcy stubbornly refused to attend to the little things that give great pleasure and cost only an effort. Later in the novel when Darcy finds himself falling in love with Elizabeth and prematurely proposing to her, she sternly rebuffs him and indicates not even the slightest interest in his intentions despite his handsomeness, affluence, and social status, responding, "and if I could *feel* gratitude, I would thank you. But I cannot—I have not desired your good opinion, and you have certainly bestowed it most unwillingly." Romance, courtship, love, and marriage demand this art of pleasing in words, manners, clothes, and favors.

Later in the novel during a visit to her aunt and uncle when Elizabeth tours Pemberley Woods, Darcy's estate, she does not expect Darcy to be at home. Of course she is naturally surprised and embarrassed at his unexpected arrival—a visitor to the home of a man whose marriage proposal she firmly rejected. However, on this occasion Darcy practices the art of pleasing. He welcomes his guests with warm cordiality, invites Elizabeth's uncle to fish in the streams on his property, initiates conversation, and conducts himself like a gentleman: "That he should even speak to her was amazing!—but to speak with such civility, to enquire after her family! Never in her life had she seen his manners so little dignified, never had he spoken with such gentleness as on this unexpected meeting." No act of civility is too small or too unimportant to neglect. Darcy's desire to extend himself and receive Elizabeth with the most obliging manners and gracious hospitality changes her first impression of him and reveals him to be a noble, chivalrous gentleman. A magnanimous man on this occasion, Darcy rises above petty grudges, cold formality, and vindictive meanness in the presence of the woman who rejected his offer of marriage. He demonstrates what Gerard Manley Hopkins calls "the handsome heart" in a poem by that name where a young boy expresses his spirit of pleasing his father with the reply "Father, what you buy me I like best" when the father asks, "But tell me, child, your choice." Pleasing others means deferring to them as Darcy does with his guests.

As Darcy's example illustrates, the art of pleasing differs from the artfulness of ingratiation. To ingratiate is to do a favor with the expectation of some benefit or advantage, to please not for the sake of bringing pleasure to another person as an end in itself but to advance one's own self-interest. Darcy, however, realizing the offices of a true gentleman, chooses to please his visitors by attending to all the needs of his guests with no ulterior motives. His whole relationship with Elizabeth improves because he proved beyond a doubt his magnanimity, his sensitivity in giving primary importance to others: ". . . when she saw him thus civil, not only to herself, but to the very relations whom he had openly disdained . . . the change was so great, and struck so forcibly on her mind, that she could hardly restrain her astonishment from being visible." Elizabeth concludes that Darcy's courteous manner—"so desirous to please, so free from self-consequence, or unbending reserve"—is disinterested because "no importance could result from the success of his endeavours." Like the bond between father and daughter in *King Lear*, the relationship between man and woman grows in harmony, friendship, and affection when persons exert concerted efforts to please one another. All relationships suffer when individuals seek their own pleasure and insist on their own way and thus disregard the humility of serving others.

The desire of pleasing, however, goes beyond the domestic ties between parents and children and beyond the romantic relations between men and women to encompass the bonds shared by all human beings by virtue of being a member of the human race. In the Homeric scenes of hospitality in the *Odyssey*, the hosts attend to all of the physical and emotional needs of travelers by providing them a warm welcome, an abundant feast, the comfort of cleaning and anointing the body, and an opportunity for conversation and storytelling. In Homer's epic, this desire to please the visitor and practice hospitality defines the essence of civilization itself, the art of living well. The barbarian, on the other hand, lacks this human sensibility of anticipating, recognizing, and responding to the needs and desires of travelers. Pleasing only himself and indulging his glut-tonous appetites, the savage Cyclops violently seizes his guests, devours their flesh, and swallows their wine in total contempt of the law of the gods that enjoins hospitality as a sacred duty. The art of pleasing, then, is a mark of humanity that obligates children and parents, men and women, and hosts and guests. As one of the elders of Phaeacia in the *Odyssey* reminds the king upon news on a visitor, "Come, raise him up and seat the stranger now, in a silver-studded chair, and tell the heralds to mix more wine for all . . . suppliants' rights are sacred." Thus the art of pleasing acknowledges the importance of another person's primary human need to be pleased and his right to happiness. The cruel words of Goneril and Regan, the cold manners of Darcy, and the crude actions of the Cyclops frustrate human interaction and violate this virtue of humanity.

In his essay "On Different Kinds of Relationships," Montaigne provides a famous example of the unwillingness to please others and of excessive indulgence of one's own whims and idiosyncrasies. In the essay Montaigne distin-guishes between his relations with friends, women, and books, explaining that ideal friendship with "another self" is rare and short-lived and that relationships with women are limited to the physical and the cloying. Rather than subject himself to tiresome company and the demands of social life, Montaigne prefers the company of the books in his library in the tower of his home to mixed company below in the household. In short, he finds sociability a waste of time and utter boredom. In Montaigne's view, attention to the constant business of pleasing and humoring others deprives him of the pleasure of perfect composure and the uninterrupted pursuit of favorite pastimes. He confesses, "I live from day to day . . . live only for myself; my purposes go no further." To Montaigne the art of pleasing amounts to no more than a silly convention that distracts from one's own comfort and convenience. He admits that he prefers the company of the books in his library to the conversation of the members of his household and the guests: "It frees me from the weight of a tedious idleness, and releases me at any moment from disagreeable company." His library on the third story he calls his "throne," his own private world where "I try to rule here absolutely, reserving this one corner from all society, conjugal, filial, and social."

From the insensitive comments or selfish behavior of Goneril and Regan, the cold snobbery of Darcy, the inhumane cruelty of the Cyclops, and the petulant complaints of Montaigne, the art of pleasing acquires the impression of a useless, sentimental, or wasteful activity that only fulfills empty social protocol but serves no practical purpose in the pursuit of comfort or pleasure. If self-interest requires the artfulness of ingratiation ("I follow him to serve my turn upon him," Shakespeare's cynical Iago remarks in *Othello*), then the art of pleasing becomes a means to an end, a matter of expediency. To elevate the art of pleasing to the status of a moral virtue or social grace as an end in itself and desirable for its own sake sounds foolishly quixotic to the cynics and critics. However, the art of pleasing confers rewards on both the one giving and the one receiving. Like all enjoyable pursuits loved and valued for the sheer joy they bring—play, friendship, beauty—the art of pleasing also redounds and bears fruit.

First, the art of pleasing inspires gratitude. As Menelaus remarks in the *Odyssey* when a servant announces the arrival of a traveler and asks if he should extend hospitality, "Just think of all the hospitality we enjoyed at the hands of other men before we made it home." Elizabeth Bennet also feels great appreciation not only for Darcy's kind attentions during her visit to his estate but also profound gratitude for his extraordinary generosity in arranging her younger sister Lydia's marriage and saving the Bennet family from the scandal of an elopement. To be pleased in a special, thoughtful way by someone moves a person to please in return. Second, the desire to please improves all human relationships and cultivates peace and amity between family members, spouses, social classes, and nations. In Shakespeare's *A Midsummer Night's Dream*, the mysterious fairies who perform their magical cures and bestow their beautiful gifts ("fairy favors") in the darkness and silence of the night to end the argument between father and daughter (Aegeus and Hermia), the quarrel between the lovers (Demetrius and Helena), and the family feud between husband and wife (Oberon and Titania). Oberon, the king of the fairies, practices this art of pleasing on every occasion and instructs his fairies to heal the wounded feelings of mortals by the gentle medicine of their kind favors. Third, the desire to please refines and civilizes human life and rescues it from selfishness, hardheartedness, and brutishness. Because Lear's ungrateful daughters refused to please their father, the king concluded that human beings and wild animals were no longer distinguishable. He protests, "I gave you all," only to have his simple request for attendants spurned by the daughters he calls "tigers" and "pelicans." Absent the art of pleasing, then charity ceases.

St. Paul's famous letter on love in 1 Corinthians (13) offers instruction in the art of pleasing as well as the meaning of love. Love does not insist on its own way. Love is never rude. Love is always patient and kind. In other words, charity always thinks of pleasing others first, not last. Charity is never irritable, unpleasant, or petulant but gentle, considerate, and obliging. Charity is not merely the giving of alms but the giving of happiness and joy to others by small favors, acts of kindness, and words of appreciation. St. Paul explained that his love of the Gospel motivated him to "become all things to all people," that is, to please others in every conceivable way, large or small.

St. Francis de Sales, renowned for his civility and *savoir-faire*, vowed in his early life always to speak to every person in attendance at social occasions, that is, to make the effort to please everyone. As Pope John Paul I in *Illustrissimi* wrote in his imaginary letter to the beloved saint, "Already as a university student, you made a vow for yourself never to avoid or curtail a conversation with anyone, no matter how unlikable and boring." Cardinal Newman's definition of a gentleman in *The Idea of a University* stated that "a gentleman is one who never inflicts pain" because he strives to be thoughtful of every person in his company, a gentleman who measures his words to avoid "whatever may cause a jolt in the minds of those with whom he is cast." Thinking always of respecting the feelings of others, a gentleman shows the utmost tact, "his great concern being to make every one at their ease and at home," Newman adds. Like St. Francis de Sales, he extends himself to everyone: "he is tender toward the bashful, gentle toward the distant, and merciful to the absurd." The art of pleasing, then, is an expression of charity and proceeds from a kind heart.

Of course the art of pleasing also encompasses man's relationship to God, the virtue of religion in which man offers worship, thanksgiving, and obedience to God as a way of honoring, remembering, and pleasing his Creator. Both the Ten Commandments and the Lord's Prayer specify the ways that man is obligated to place God's wishes and God's will above his own desires and pleasures. "If you love me, you will keep my commandments," Christ taught his disciples. The Beatitudes also express the various ways that human beings can please God and evoke the word "Blessed." However, just as it is necessary to learn manners first in order to exercise morals and just as it is necessary to love neighbor in order to love God, it is paramount for human beings to learn to please parents, children, spouses, and guests as a social and moral habit that naturally instills the willingness and joy of loving and pleasing God.

CHAPTER SIX

The Lost Art of Courtship

IN WESTERN literature the pursuit of wisdom is often compared to the quest for love. In the Book of Proverbs, for example, the father addressing his son personifies wisdom as feminine as he counsels him, "Wisdom cries aloud in the street; in the markets she raises her voice; on the top of the wall she cries out," and "Do not forsake her, and she will keep you; love her, and she will guard you." (*Proverbs* 1:20–21; 4:6). In Boethius's *The Consolation of Philosophy* Lady Philosophy, described as a woman of "awe-inspiring appearance, her eyes burning and keen beyond the usual power of men," embodies the summit of human wisdom attainable by reason. In Fielding's *Tom Jones* the young protagonist's desire for his beloved Sophia ("wisdom" in Greek) corresponds to his education in prudence. In these examples the person who desires wisdom or seeks truth must woo her in the way a man courts a woman he loves and hopes to marry.

The seeker of wisdom must, first, behold the venerable lady as infinitely desirable, as beautiful and lovable for her own sake. "Prize her highly, and she will exalt you; she will honor you if you embrace her," the father urges his son (Proverbs 4:8).

The lover too views his beloved with contemplative wonder and feels strong attraction at the miracle of beauty. However, after being moved to admire and feeling the allure, the lover must express a desire for the beloved that leads to pursuit, the wooing of the woman that courtship initiates. Wisdom, however, demands proof of the student's worthiness in the form of devotion, steadfastness, and self-discipline. The beloved also requires attention, single-mindedness, and commitment. Luke-warmness and half-heartedness never win the prize of wisdom or love. In addition to appreciating the desirability and appeal of wisdom and love as great gifts or pearls of great price and exercising constant diligence in the attainment of the goal, the passionate student and the ardent lover must demonstrate a purity of motive and sincerity of heart for their love to be requited. Wisdom—truth in its purity—does not offer herself to the impure who desire her with selfish motives or with worldly intentions. She does not respond to anyone who does not love her for her own sake as intrinsically good and beautiful as she is. The beloved woman likewise needs to be won and convinced—all her reservations removed—that the man wooing her truly loves her for the special person she is rather than merely flatters her with an insincere "I love you." Purity of heart without ulterior motives and honorable intentions without any taint of deceit or self-interest touch the heart of the beloved to reciprocate, surrender, and say "yes."

Courtship, then, is not rash, impulsive, or impatient. Wisdom and love are rewards that honor effort, dedication, and fidelity. It takes time to reveal one's intentions, to determine the state of one's heart, to prove one's worthiness, to feel love's growth, and to listen to the voice of conscience. Every stage in this courtship from beginning to end plays a vital part. If the lover takes no interest, exerts no effort, and never initiates the pursuit, then of course Lady Philosophy and the Beautiful Woman remain inaccessible, removed, and aloof. If the lover shows some attention but loses fervor because he lacks incentive, momentum, or conviction, he fails to attain his prize. Likewise, if he proceeds too hastily without allowing love to follow its normal development, he fails to respect the woman's right to decide her suitability, to judge his worthiness, and to consult her own heart. If the course of true love flows naturally and follows all the stages of courtship—attraction, desire, diligence, patience, and constancy—then a small beginning culminates in an astonishing surprise and a tiny seed of love blossoms into the fruitfulness of love's harvest.

While in the past arranged marriages and political alliances often frustrated the art of courtship and the mysterious flowering of true love as C.S. Lewis's *The Allegory of Love* argues, the modern habit of "living together" in cohabitation and with contraception also destroys the romance and wonder of love's quiet, slow revelation and its providential mystery. Wisdom is so valuable that it must be earned by rising to its heights; it does not condescend. As the father says of wisdom, "She is more precious than jewels, and nothing you desire can compare with her." (*Proverbs* 5:15). Love too is a sublime ideal, and it demands an arduous ascent and the discipline of virtue. Lady Philosophy, described by Boethius as at times touching "the very sky with the top of her head" and raising herself even higher until she was "lost to human sight," never lowers herself. Both Lady Philosophy and the Beautiful Woman do not compromise their principles, lower their standards, or cheapen their character. They uplift the student or the lover to an ideal of excellence and selflessness that demands some form of self-sacrifice or self-denial that rewards him generously for his conquest of sloth, lust, or selfishness. Just as Lady Philosophy resists the sophist who misuses knowledge or manipulates her for his own self-serving ends of power, wealth, or pleasure, the Beloved Woman does not yield to the flatterer or to the seducer. Only the noble, the honorable, and the pure attract the true, the good, and beautiful. Cohabitation seizes the beloved in a form of robbery, and the beloved prostitutes herself as love degenerates into lust and adultery. Likewise, if Lady Philosophy requited those who exploit her rather than love and serve her, she would debase herself and lose her glory and stature.

Jane Austen's novels especially portray the lost art of courtship and the mystery of love it unveils. These stories portray romances that feign true courtship in the rush to achieve matrimony by a fixed deadline, couples that initiate courtship but prematurely abandon it because of the absence of fervor and constancy, attachments that ignore the protocol of courtship and plunge into elopement and cohabitation, and relationships that cooperate with the design of true love from courtship to marriage. Because true courtship requires time and patience for love to pass through its proper stages and culminate in the happiness of marriage, it cannot be limited to a prescribed period of time. On the other hand, courtship as a preparation for marriage does not signify an indefinite perpetuity with no end in sight. Courtship represents the normal time required for the seed of love to grow to fruition, for the soul, mind, heart, and character of the man and woman to be known and revealed. A courtship that begins and stops because of the intrusions of others' opinions and influences fails to enjoy the entire period necessary for love's growth. A relationship that ignores the propriety of courtship and flouts its conventions disregards the role of time in forming the sensibilities of the heart and confuses the sentiments of love with erotic desires. True courtship, on the other hand, does not require a fixed date. It is not easily distracted by outside forces. It never views the beloved as a mere object of pleasure, as a symbol of social respectability, or as a mere source of economic security but as the essence of goodness and beauty.

In *Pride and Prejudice* the officious, pompous Mr. Collins visits the Bennet family to marry one of the older daughters because his aristocratic patroness, Lady Catherine de Bourgh, urges the Anglican clergyman to follow social convention and seek marriage for the sake of image and prestige. Thus he suddenly announces his arrival to the Bennet family and declares his intentions in a letter that astonishes everyone: "Having now a good house and very sufficient income, he intended to marry; and in seeking a reconciliation with the Longbourn family he had a wife in view, as he meant to chuse one of the daughters, if he found them as handsome and amiable as they were represented by common report." During this brief visit of a few weeks he had originally intended to marry the oldest daughter Jane, but Mr. Bingley is currently courting the eldest Bennet daughter. Mr. Collins then offers marriage to Elizabeth, the second oldest who firmly rejects his proposal because she finds his affected manners and insensitive, heavy-handed approach to marriage to be the silly behavior of a man who lacks all tact and good taste. Elizabeth can barely restrain her laughing when Mr. Collins proposes: "My reasons for marrying are, first, that I think it a right thing for every clergyman . . . to set the example in his parish. Secondly, that I am convinced it will add very greatly to my happiness; and thirdly . . . that it is the particular advice and recommendation of the very noble lady whom I have the honour of calling patroness." Frustrated at his failure to win the hand of either Jane or Elizabeth, Collins then turns his attention to Charlotte Lucas and a few days later proposes again to yet another woman, one who accepts his hasty offer—a marriage without the foundation of courtship, without the experience of falling in love, and without esteem, admiration, or mutual respect. Shocked at Charlotte's easy acceptance of Collins' perfunctory proposal, Elizabeth loses respect for her dear friend who compromises moral principle for financial security and social approval to escape the stigma of old maid. As Charlotte once explained to Elizabeth, she was not at all "romantic" about marriage: "Happiness in marriage is entirely a matter of chance . . . ; and it is better to know as little as possible of the defects of the person with whom you are to pass your life." As the novel later reveals, a marriage without courtship frustrates the romance of falling in love, and without courtship and love a conventional marriage settles into mere formality or mutual tolerance—a situation depicted in Elizabeth's visit to the married couple where Charlotte's clever arrangement of the home forces her husband to keep at a distance in his library far removed from the dining room.

Pride and Prejudice also presents a relationship that begins in courtship but soon falters because of the lover's lack of ardor and conviction. After the Netherfield ball Bingley and Jane are naturally attracted to each other. Mr. Bingley's personal interest in Jane, his special attentions, and his frequent dances with her convince many observers, especially Mrs. Bennet, that Bingley has initiated a courtship that is destined for marriage. However, Bingley's auspicious romance with Jane soon flounders because his more socially prominent family neither approves of the Bennets' middle-class status nor recommends the manners of Mrs. Bennet or the conduct of the younger sisters. Thus a promising match between an ideal, compatible couple with admirable manners and morals fails because of the meddlesomeness of snobbish sisters and the officiousness of Bingley's friend Mr. Darcy. A letter written by Caroline Bingley to Jane coyly insinuates that her brother's sudden departure to London will encourage his engagement with Georgiana Darcy—"an event that will secure the happiness of so many." The art of courtship, then, demands perseverance and constancy in the pursuit of the beloved lest interferences, impediments, and unwarranted opinions mar the steady growth of love. Jane remains a cherished prize of love, but Bingley's fickle nature reduces his strong desire into lukewarm interest as he temporarily allows family biases to stifle the inspirations of the heart. As Elizabeth observes, "Miss Bingley sees her brother is in love with you, and wants him to marry Miss Darcy."

The novel also portrays an impulsive elopement and a hasty marriage without benefit of courtship or propriety. Lydia Bennet's flirtatious interest in the soldiers and George Wickham's irresponsible habits of squandering money, spreading lies, and exploiting others tempt the couple to elope, cohabit, and ignore the formality of courtship and engagement and the moral norms of matrimony. Shocked and offended by this social and moral disgrace, Mr. Bennet travels to locate the couple and resolve this embarrassment that has tainted the family's reputation of respectability. However, it is only with Mr. Darcy's noble intercession that the scandalous affair concludes in marriage—the magnanimity of Darcy paying the wedding expenses and providing Wickham an allowance under the condition that he and Lydia wed and end this humiliation. As this example demonstrates, elopement, cohabitation, and a rushed marriage do not augur the bliss of marital love. Lydia tempts Wickham, Wickham seduces Lydia, lust rules, and an official marriage follows that only removes dishonor from the Bennet name but bodes ill for the shameless couple who violate both the moral laws and social conventions that govern marriage. Naturally this embarrassment cheapens the whole quality of romantic love because Wickham failed to honor and woo Lydia with chivalry and in accordance with family expectations and moral principles and because she prostituted herself to the demands of Wickham's selfish desires. In his violation of courtship Wickham did not win the hand of Lydia, prove his worthiness, act honorably, or cherish her as "more precious than jewels"

While depicting hasty, perfunctory courtships like Collins' proposal to Charlotte Lucas, tepid courtships like Bingley's uncommitted romance to Jane, and the omission of courtship in Wickham and Lydia's reckless elopement, *Pride and Prejudice* also illuminates the mystery of this important social art. Despite offending the young ladies and their parents at the Netherfield ball in his refusal to dance or converse and his contemptuous remark that he found no woman elegant enough to engage his company, Darcy finds himself unwillingly attracted to Elizabeth and cannot resist proposing marriage to her— to a woman who had already arrived at her final judgment of this prideful gentleman: "to her he was only the man who made himself agreeable no where, and who had not thought her handsome enough to dance with." Without any of the natural movements of courtship, without proof of his honor or purity of intention, and without winning the heart of the beloved by any proof of nobility or goodness, Darcy dares to offer marriage with the presumption that Elizabeth would welcome the proposal of a wealthy, handsome gentleman with gratitude. Furthermore, Darcy, objecting to the indiscreet manners of Mrs. Bennet and the younger daughters, has dissuaded his friend Bingley from courting Jane and marrying into the family. Thus Elizabeth, whose first impressions of Darcy already have created ill will, sternly rejects Darcy's premature, awkward proposal of marriage: "It is natural that obligation should be felt, and if I could *feel* gratitude, I would now thank you. But I cannot—I have never desired your good opinion, and you have certainly bestowed it most unwillingly." Elizabeth then castigates him for his role in discouraging Bingley's courtship with Jane: "Had not my own feelings decided against you, had they been indifferent, or had they been favourable, do you think that any consideration would tempt me to accept the man, who has been the means of ruining, perhaps for ever, the happiness of a most beloved sister?" Again the failure of romantic courtship prohibits the realization of true love. Darcy neither acknowledges Elizabeth at the ball with a compliment, a friendly word, or an offer to dance nor courts her like a gentleman. Darcy never proves his worthiness to the beloved and does nothing to earn the prize of love—the very *raison d'etre* of courtship.

However, after the passage of several months, Elizabeth, on

a tour of Pemberley Woods with her aunt and uncle Mr. and Mrs. Gardiner, finds herself admiring both the beautiful woods and the elegant interior of the home, Darcy's estate: "She had never seen a place for which nature had done more, or where natural beauty had been so little counteracted by an awkward taste"—a powerful impression that moves her to utter, "to be mistress of Pemberley might be something!" Assuming that Darcy is normally absent from the country during this time of the year, Elizabeth feels awkward embarrassment at the news of his unexpected arrival. Their embarrassing exchange at his earlier proposal, her resentment at Darcy's role in frustrating Jane's romance, and Darcy's air of superiority at the Netherfield ball have disposed Elizabeth to dispel any thoughts of friendship or romance with him. However, on this occasion Darcy receives his visitors with warm cordiality, welcomes his guests with gracious hospitality, and acts like a magnanimous gentleman who holds no petty grudges toward the woman who angrily rejected his offer of marriage. Elizabeth finds herself admiring the man she earlier begrudged: "That he should even speak to her was amazing!—but to speak with such civility, to enquire after her family! Never in her life had she seen his manners so little dignified, never had he spoken with such gentleness as on this unexpected meeting." This occasion at Pemberley Woods provides Elizabeth a second "first impression" of Darcy that hints of romantic courtship. Darcy is courteous, attentive, pleasing, and most interested in conversing with Elizabeth and changing his conduct to win her respect. Elizabeth wonders, "Why is he so altered? From what can it proceed? It cannot be for *my* sake that his manners are thus softened. My reproofs at Hunsford could not work such a change as this." Of course it is for her sake that Darcy acts the part of the perfect gentleman who desires her approval and admiration as he testifies shortly before their engagement: "My object then… was to shew you, by every civility in my power, that I was not so mean as to resent the past; and I hoped to obtain your forgiveness, to lessen your ill opinion, by letting you see that your opinions had been attended to." Like wisdom "more precious than gold" and like Lady Philosophy in her great height who refuse to sacrifice their high ideals, Elizabeth Bennet does not stoop to the level of marriage for the sake of financial benefits or for social reputation. Darcy must rise to meet her expectations of manners and morals in an honorable gentleman. In true courtship the beloved inspires the chivalry and magnanimity of a noble man who serves her with disinterested motives.

Although Darcy never deigns to flatter Elizabeth before or after the episode at Pemberley or affects good manners to ingratiate Elizabeth before attempting a second proposal, he feels an obligation to intercede on behalf of the Bennet family when the youngest daughter Lydia elopes with George Wickham. A young man adopted and educated by Darcy's father, Wickham plotted to marry Darcy's sister to inherit part of the family fortune. Feeling guilt about not familiarizing others with the dishonorable past of Wickham, Darcy senses a duty to preserve the Bennet family name from disgrace and to persuade the couple to end their infamous affair. When the good news reaches the Bennets that Lydia is married, that Wickham's debts have been paid, and that the whole shameful incident has been settled, the Bennets give credit to their uncle Mr. Gardiner for saving the family's honor by paying Wickham's enormous debts to overcome his objections to marriage. However, in a confidential letter to Elizabeth, Mrs. Gardiner discloses to her niece the real benefactor: Mr. Darcy insisted on making all the financial settlements at his own expense because, allegedly, "It was owing to him, to his reserve, and want of proper consideration, that Wickham's character had been so misunderstood. . . ." Yet Mrs. Gardiner adds, "your uncle would not have yielded, if we had not given him credit for *another interest* in the affair." In short, Darcy's love for Elizabeth inspired his generosity. In the words of the proverb "Do good by stealth and blush to find it fame," Darcy gives without expecting to receive or to gain attention, yet the secret is known and eventually communicated to Elizabeth. A true courtship between Darcy and Elizabeth now has a firm basis: he treats her with manners, he respects her family, he is willing to please her in small ways and in great matters, he will humble himself to accommodate Elizabeth's wishes, and he will serve her with honor and chivalry.

Thus like the student who seeks wisdom or serves Lady Philosophy by elevating himself rather than forcing her to lower herself, Darcy follows the journey of true courtship by rising to the highest standards of excellence to win his beloved. He finds Elizabeth attractive and irresistible despite his initial reluctance: "Darcy had never been so bewitched by any woman as he was by her. He really believed, that were it not for the inferiority of her connections, he should be in some danger." Even though Elizabeth dispels the idea of matrimony when Darcy prematurely proposes without wooing and winning her heart, Darcy does not lose all interest as seen in his special attentiveness to Elizabeth at Pemberley Woods and in his intention to make reparations by conducting himself like a perfect gentleman. From their accidental meeting at Pemberley Woods Darcy begins a proper courtship that redeems his earlier flaws when he confesses "how insufficient were all my pretensions to please a woman worthy of being pleased." For Elizabeth's sake he cultivates habits and virtues to prove his worthiness of her favor. As Mrs. Gardiner remarks, "I was never more surprised than by his behaviour to us. It was more than civil; it was really attentive; and there was no necessity for such attention. His acquaintance with Elizabeth was trifling." Darcy's sense of *noblesse oblige* in arranging the marriage of Wickham and Lydia and his liberality in paying all the debts as an incentive for the couple to marry reflect Darcy's pure love for Elizabeth—a revelation that all true courtship seeks as proof that the man loves the woman for her own sake, as "better than gold" and "more precious than jewels." As Elizabeth comprehends the whole series of events, "Her heart did whisper, that he had done it for her." Now that Darcy has noticed the striking beauty and elegance of Elizabeth, courted her with manners and morals, proven his honorable intentions, and demonstrated his chivalry and integrity, the beloved surrenders and realizes she is indeed in love for all the right reasons: "She began now to comprehend that he was exactly the man, who, in disposition and talents, would most suit her."

When courtship acquires the reputation of a quaint custom of the past or of a perfunctory formality, the progress of love's growth does not run its true course as a romantic story. When courtship is accelerated for the sake of convenience or ease, the knowledge of the heart, the poetry of love, is absent. When courtship begins favorably but ends abruptly, it suffers an unnatural termination that robs love of its mysterious and dramatic surprises. When courtship is flouted for the sake of elopement or cohabitation, love loses its glorious climax and ecstatic happy ending. But when courtship is pursued in the way of a student seeking wisdom or desiring Lady Philosophy, the lover wonders at the magnificence or greatness of love and cherishes it as a pearl, a prize, and a gift made it heaven for the pure in heart, "a tree of life to those who lay hold of her." (*Proverbs* 3:18).

The Lost Art of Tasteful Dressing or Proper Attire

By Mitchell Kalpakgian

CLOTHING is both practical and aesthetic. It serves the utilitarian purpose of protecting the body from rain and snow, and it adorns and dignifies human beings by presenting them in an attractive appearance that reflects their divinity and nobility and expresses their individual beauty, charm, or taste. Clothing, then, is symbolic. That is, the body reveals the soul; the outer, visible beauty of the human form manifests the hidden mystery of the person or the condition of the spirit. Just as the eyes and complexion hint of the illness of the sick, the clothing, style, and taste of men and women make statements about themselves and send messages to others. Human clothing, thus, serves several purposes. First, besides protection from cold and heat, it asserts the self-respect of a person who projects himself as an image of God rather than a ragamuffin or tramp approaching the lot of animals—a person rejoicing in the dignity of his manhood or womanhood. Second, proper clothing also communicates an attitude toward others, the desire of pleasing company and the thoughtfulness of not giving offense by way of negligence of the amenities of social life. Third, the art of tasteful dress creates a beautiful atmosphere and uplifts ordinary life from the prosaic to the poetic as it adorns the black and white colors of common life with brighter tones and varied combinations that distinguish festive occasions. Finally, the quality of proper dress defines a culture as civilized, refined, modest, or polished as it forms an ideal, establishes a custom, and captures a tone that pervades an entire society and sets a standard. In Shakespeare's play *Hamlet* captures this aesthetic, moral, exalted dimension of human nature with his famous statement:

> What a piece of work is a man! How noble in reason! How infinite in faculty! In form and moving how express and admirable! In action how like an angel! In apprehension how like a god! The beauty of the world! The paragon of animals! (II. ii. 315–319)

Language and clothes generally fall into three major categories: the designation of formal, standard, and colloquial in language usage and the category of ceremonious occasions, business attire, and casual clothing with regard to dress. These are not arbitrary, invented classifications but natural divisions inherent in the structure of reality. Human experience consists of high, solemn, festive occasions like the celebration of the divine liturgy on a Sunday, weddings, funeral masses, and other formal events. Human experience also involves the business of ordinary life in the workaday world and in the management of a home and the care of children. Life also provides times of leisure, relaxation, and play distinct from high occasions and the obligations of work. A human life acknowledges these natural distinctions that encompass the universal experience of mankind and distinguishes between them with a use of language and clothing that clarifies the vital differences between high and low, work and play, formal and casual. Just as lexicographers identify the level of particular words as archaic, colloquial, substandard, slang, or obscure, human dress also clarifies the various occasions of life as religious or secular, as grand or ordinary, as business or play. The preservation of these normal differences and natural distinctions upholds the manners and mores of civilized life. The destruction of these different gradations of speech and dress, however, leads to a form of leveling or reductionism that robs human life of beauty and wonder in its many forms. Just as language expresses beauty or grandeur in the form of poetry or epic, clothing also radiates a splendor or grace that declares elegance and stylishness. Man's use of words and clothes that can range from the elegant to the vulgar can either elevate him or lower him, portraying him as either "a little lower than the angels" or on a level with animals. In a famous speech from *King Lear*, Shakespeare illuminates this critical distinction when the king excoriates his two ungrateful daughters for obliterating the very distinctions that separate human beings from animals:

> Oh, reason not the need. Our basest beggars
> Are in the poorest things superfluous.
> Allow not nature more than nature needs,
> Man's life's as cheap as beast's. Thou art a lady.
> If only to go warm were gorgeous,
> Why, nature needs not what thou gorgeous wear'st,
> Which scarcely keeps thee warm. (II. iv. 267-273)

In other words, man needs more than the barest necessities for mere survival. Lear's daughters do not dress only to keep warm but also to look gorgeous. Every human being is entitled to the accessories that serve no utilitarian purpose, the "extras" that ennoble, dignify, or adorn the human body. Jewelry and neckties do not keep a person warm but enhance a person's sense of self-respect. By complaining, denying the king his attendants, and protesting that his fifty or twenty-five servants are redundant and unnecessary ("What need one?"), Lear's daughters are reducing a stately king and a venerable man to a beggar. They are stripping him of the royal apparel that establishes his authority, identity, and humanity. Thus clothing is not a trivial, insignificant matter as it can heighten the pageant of life's beauty or flatten life to humdrum existence, allow a person to uphold his humanity or deprive him of his dignity.

Propriety in the use of language and in the matter of clothing expresses social graciousness, courtesy, and manners that elevate human existence into civilized life. Speech and dress represent forms of respecting and pleasing others by forms of address that honor the sensibilities of human beings and adorn human life with "the poetry of conduct" to use C.S. Lewis's phrase. When these distinctions between the formal and informal and between the dignified and casual are blurred so that people dress informally for high occasions and wear casual clothing for ceremonious events, the sense of beauty diminishes as bland homogeneity or promiscuous appearance replace style and grace. The art of pleasing others—a social obligation and a charitable act—requires attention to matters of dress lest human life become drab and dingy instead of attractive and charming. In Orwell's *1984*, Winston laments the disappearance of femininity that Big Brother's totalitarian government has forced upon the population—a cultural revolution in which women have lost their attractiveness because of a disdain for stylish feminine clothing and appearance. As Julia says defiantly to Winston, "I'm going to get hold of a real woman's frock from somewhere and wear it instead of these bloody trousers. I'll wear silk stockings and high-heeled shoes! In this room I'm going to be a woman, not a Party comrade." The classless society of Oceania and the sexless androgyny indoctrinated into the citizens in Orwell's novel instill a disregard for the art of tasteful clothing for the sake of utilitarian practicality, and the consequence is a monotonous life never refreshed by the radiance of the beautiful. Winston remarks, "It struck him that the truly characteristic thing about modern life was not its cruelty and insecurity, but simply its bareness, its dinginess, its listlessness." On the other hand, wherever proper attire is valued as an art of pleasing, beauty abounds and transforms the quality of daily life from bare and dingy to sparkling and elegant as Jane Austen's novels illustrate. For example, in *Mansfield Park* the heroine Fanny Price—the epitome of good taste and modest elegance—who always seeks to please receives this compliment from her cousin Edmund as she dresses for a ball. When she asks, "I hope you do not think me too fine," Edmund replies, "A woman can never be too fine while she is all in white. No, I see no finery about you; nothing but what is perfectly proper." Proper clothing, then, heightens occasions with the magnificence of beauty just as careless, lackluster dress deprives social life of its grace.

The art of tasteful dressing, however, does not mean glamorous, luxurious, or expensive clothing dictated by advertising, and it does not mean the blind following of silly trends that dictate conformity. At the same time the art of proper attire avoids the odd, eccentric, and archaic that detracts from a person's appearance rather than enhances it. In *Introduction to a Devout Life* St. Francis de Sales explains the ideal of appropriate apparel with these guidelines. A person with good taste avoids affectation, vanity, and frivolity, inclining "always to the side of simplicity and modesty." A person with a sense of propriety remembers that appropriate dress honors the dignity of those in attendance: "It is a sort of contempt of those you associate with to frequent their company in unbecoming attire." The art of tasteful dressing cultivates a sense of the aesthetic that adorns the quality of human life and rescues it from monotonous dullness: "For my part, I would have devout people, whether men or women, always the best dressed in a group but the least pompous and affected. As the proverb says, I would have them adorned with grace, decency, and dignity." St. Thomas Aquinas's classic definition of the beautiful, *"Id quod visum placet"* (That which being seen pleases) relates the beautiful to the visual and the sensory—a form of pleasing others and delighting the sense of sight. When these guidelines are flouted as people dress for the sake of casual comfort or ostentation or ignore the sensibilities of others and violate simplicity, modesty, or decorum, the joy or dignity of the occasion suffers as a social or ceremonious event appears as just another commonplace occasion. Throughout all of the festive banquet scenes in the *Odyssey* and *Iliad*, Homer always records the beautiful clothing of the participants. On the shield of Achilles the festive adornments and the beautiful clothing capture the art of living well: "Here young boys and girls, beauties courted with costly gifts of oxen, danced and danced. . . . And the girls wore robes of linen light and flowing, the boys wore finespun tunics rubbed with a gloss of oil, the girls were crowned with a bloom of fresh garlands, the boys swung golden daggers on silver belts." As Joseph Pieper explains in *Leisure: The Basis of Culture*, without Sundays, holidays, and festivities to punctuate the world of work and the course of the year, man—burdened by the repetition of work—forgets to "stand erect and walk again" and be renewed in the spirit.

The significance and symbolism of clothes should neither be exaggerated like the king in "The Emperor's New Clothes" nor minimized as Montaigne does in his essay "On the Custom of Wearing of Clothes." In Hans Andersen's famous story, the vain king always gazing into the mirror to admire himself seeks to impress others and glamorize his image. Andersen writes, "He was so passionately fond of clothes that he spent all his money and time in dressing up. He cared nothing for his army, nor for going to the theatre, nor for driving his carriage among the people—except as a chance for showing off his latest outfit. He had a coat for every hour of the day." Of course, as the child announces during the procession of the king through the streets with everyone pretending to compliment him even though he is wearing no clothes, "He's got nothing on!" The purpose of clothes is not to pretend, deceive, or conceal but to intimate the essence of the person—the taste, judgment, and manners—the outer appearance revealing the inner being in the way that eyes are the window of the soul. As Squire Allworthy advised Tom Jones in Fielding's novel, one must not only "be good" but also "appear to be good" so that the correspondence between outward behavior and inner character complement each other. One does not light a lamp and then hide it under a bushel as Christ taught when he enjoined, "Let your light so shine before men that they may see your good works and glorify your Father in heaven." This light does not exclude clothing and appearance. Carelessness about propriety gives false first impressions and distorts the truth rather than revealing it. When clothes are flaunted in ostentatious display like the Emperor's pomposity, then outward image replaces moral character, and clothes signify only superficial appearance rather than a true sign.

Likewise, just as vain, affected dress leads to style without substance when clothing deceives—the wolf dressed in sheep's clothing—the contempt for tasteful dress also breeds vices. Michel de Montaigne in his essay "On the Custom of Wearing Clothes" regards clothing as no more than the idiosyncrasy of custom. He observes that just as all animals and plants have "sufficient covering to protect them from the assaults of the weather," human beings also have the capacity to adapt and inure themselves to the elements with little or no clothing as many primitive people illustrate: "For some of those peoples who have no knowledge of clothing live in climates roughly similar to ours, and, moreover, our own delicate parts are those which are always exposed." If the face is exposed in all weather with no harmful effects, argues Montaigne, why does the rest of the body require "breeches and petticoats" when men in Turkey "go naked out of religious devotion"? From his reading of Herodotus, Montaigne comments, "of those left dead on the field, the Egyptians had incomparably harder skulls than the Persians because the latter invariably covered their heads, first with bonnets and then with turbans, while the former were close-shaven from infancy and went bare-headed." In short,

Montaigne views the custom of clothing as a silly, arbitrary convention with no rational basis in human nature or reality. Clothes hardly serve any practical, aesthetic, or symbolic purpose, neither ennobling human nature, beautifying the body, pleasing others, nor creating an atmosphere of elegance or grace. For Montaigne, unlike St. Francis de Sales, clothing has no ideal or norm that dictates good taste or propriety because dress is merely a matter of individual taste, and of tastes there is no disputing as the Latin saying indicates: "*De gustibus non est disputandum.*" While most Frenchmen display motley colors in their clothing, Montaigne avoids this variety: "I seldom wear anything but black or white." And while most French laborers wear shirts open at the collar, Montaigne "cannot bear to be unbuttoned and unlaced." For Montaigne clothing, then, is relative—no more than a matter of individual opinion.

Unfortunately, the postmodern American world has adopted a view of clothing that resembles the views of the Emperor in Anderson's story and the outlook of Montaigne more than the attitude of St. Francis de Sales. Whereas de Sales advised men and women to be "the best dressed in a group," he also warned against pomp, frivolity, and affectation—faults that a consumer culture breeds by its glamorous advertising, brand names, and designer labels that especially appeal to youth culture. Whereas de Sales upheld certain norms like "simplicity and modesty" or ideals like "grace, decency, and dignity" as a paradigm for good taste, the modern practice of body piercings and tattoos exemplifies Montaigne's notion of dress as individualistic and idiosyncratic, no more than a matter of indisputable personal preference: "Anything goes." The Christian virtue of modesty in dress is most notoriously flouted by the female swimwear that abounds in all the beaches of modern America and in the suggestive, risque apparel that film and television present as titillation. Whereas de Sales counsels, "be neat, Philothea, don't allow anything negligent and careless to be about you," church attendance in many places of worship on Sunday reflects indifference, casualness, and sloth about the etiquette of tasteful clothing appropriate for the place and occasion, for more and more types of casual, leisurely dress— T-shirts, shorts, beach sandals, sweatshirts—appear to supplant the norm of dignified formality. This indiscriminate habit of careless dressing with total disregard for the feelings of others not only detracts from the occasion and offends sensibilities but also lacks the tact of avoiding offense. Disregard for propriety forms the habit of insensibility that ignores the finer feelings of men and women. Indifference, negligence, and carelessness in matters of speech, dress, or obligations manifest the sin of sloth. As Chaucer writes in "The Parson's Tale," "For sloth does no such diligence; it carries out all things in a disgruntled way, peevishly, slackly, and with excuses, slovenliness, laziness, and unwillingness."

The art of tasteful clothing, then, is a civilized norm that cultivates the habit of discrimination and good judgment. It is not a matter of blindly following the rage of fashion in which everyone in "The Emperor's New Clothes" copies the other person in the way the entire court from the king to the ministers to the officials to the attendants all pretend the king looks magnificent in the clothing that he does not wear. The art of proper apparel transcends the dress code of particular professions and involves more than meticulous conformity to rigid rules and regulations that demand exact obedience as in military dress. Because propriety in dress considers "the various circumstances of time, rank, company, and occasion," to cite de Sales, it is an art rather than a method and assesses the entire situation. As he explains, penitential seasons, holidays, weddings, funerals have different requirements. Young maidens, married women, and widows occupy different situations in life. Princes, dignitaries, friends, and family members represent different ranks of company that deserve their appropriate dress. These decisions of proper clothing consider the specific details and the particular persons and judge according to an ideal, norm, or standard that surpasses the dictates of fashion or profession. Likewise, proper dress is not a mere matter of self-expression or individual opinion, taste, or preference that ignores the canons of decorum. It is the art of the golden mean that avoids both the servile imitation of the fashionable and the chic and the careless indifference to the thoughts and feelings of others. This art of discrimination weighs and balances delicate matters to achieve the right touch and the perfect note so that appearance does not denote empty show, cold plainness, or eccentric self-expression. In de Sales' words, the norm of proper dress illustrates the virtue of moderation: "St. Louis says in a few words that 'each one should dress according to his condition, so that the wise and the good have no reason to complain that you do too much or young people say you do too little.'"

Without this knowledge of discrimination and good taste which proper clothing instills, human life undergoes distortion, and civilization loses one of its most refining amenities. The symbolic nature of clothing declares that the beautiful incarnates the good and the true. These three terms, called "the transcendentals" by St. Thomas Aquinas, are interchangeable according to the Angelic Doctor: no beauty, no goodness; no goodness, no truth; no truth, no beauty. As Cardinal Newman explains in *The Idea of the University*, loving virtue for its own sake illustrates that "this love-inspiring quality in virtue is its beauty" and "the most natural beauty in the world is honesty and moral truth; for all beauty is truth." When clothes do not matter, then truth and goodness do not matter as mere opinion exalts itself as the ultimate authority. St. Paul writes, "The invisible things of God are known by the things that are visible," and the Psalmist announces, "The heavens are telling the glory of God, and the firmament proclaims his handiwork." The beautiful, true, and good are incarnate in the visible creation. If dress is merely the requirement of a uniform or a gesture of individualism, human dignity suffers, the desire to please is lacking, and the highest aesthetic ideal diminishes. Homogeneity replaces distinctiveness as Orwell demonstrates in *1984*. Leveling and egalitarianism supplant hierarchy or "degree" as King Lear's speech on clothing verifies. The bland and the nondescript pose as the best and the excellent. And the social purpose of clothing as a gesture of graciousness and elegance—man at his best and highest—is sacrificed for the view of clothing as utilitarian expediency, personal convenience, or ostentatious show—man at the lowest common denominator. If clothes do not capture a sense of the beautiful, then truth also suffers because the beautiful reflects the true and the good. Wherever the canons of good taste and proper attire fail as ideal standards, the beauty of truth and the goodness of beauty also fade as ideology and relativism substitute current fashions in thought and dress for the time-honored canons of civilization that St. Francis de Sales summarized as "grace, decency, and dignity."

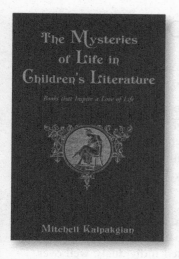

NEUMANN PRESS

◀ The Mysteries of Life in Children's Literature

Books that Inspire a Love of Life

Mitchell Kalpakgian

Fairy tales and myths have enriched childhood for centuries. In between "Once upon a time" and "happily ever after" we embark on adventures that seem an eternity away from our everyday lives. Yet nothing could be further from the truth.

In *The Mysteries of Life in Children's Literature*, journey through a treasury of beloved fables and folk tales and discover the wisdom hiding within. In an age that rejects moral absolutes, children's literature restores the meaning of good and evil, beautiful and ugly, normal and abnormal—and helps us see the nature of our world more clearly than we ever have before. *208 pgs.*

978-0-911845-99-0 Paperbound

The Three Marks of Manhood ▶

How to be Priest, Prophet and King of Your Family

G.C. Dilsaver

Christian husbands and fathers are called by God to a familial headship which is not one of old and obsolete dominance over wife and children which rose out of pagan notions of male superiority. Dilsaver promotes a new and untainted patriarchy in which the husband's ultimate authority is rooted in Christ's example of humility and self sacrificing love. *The Three Marks of Manhood* can help Christian families realize their identity to the fullest—empowering them to resist the encroachment of secular culture. *198 pgs.*

978-0-89555-904-3 Paperbound

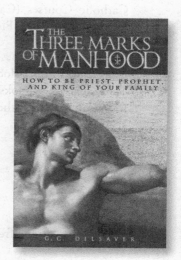

TANBooks.com • (800) 437-5876

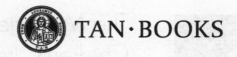

TAN·BOOKS

TAN Books was founded in 1967 to preserve the spiritual, intellectual and liturgical traditions of the Catholic Church. At a critical moment in history TAN kept alive the great classics of the Faith and drew many to the Church. In 2008 TAN was acquired by Saint Benedict Press. Today TAN continues its mission to a new generation of readers.

From its earliest days TAN has published a range of booklets that teach and defend the Faith. Through partnerships with organizations, apostolates, and mission-minded individuals, well over 10 million TAN booklets have been distributed.

More recently, TAN has expanded its publishing with the launch of Catholic calendars and daily planners—as well as Bibles, fiction, and multimedia products through its sister imprints Catholic Courses (CatholicCourses.com) and Saint Benedict Press (SaintBenedictPress.com).

Today TAN publishes over 500 titles in the areas of theology, prayer, devotions, doctrine, Church history, and the lives of the saints. TAN books are published in multiple languages and found throughout the world in schools, parishes, bookstores and homes.